AFTER ANGOLA
The War over Southern Africa

AFTER ANGOLA
The War Over
Southern Africa

Generously Donated to
The Frederick Douglass Institute
By Professor Jesse Moore
Fall 2000

The Role of the Big Powers
COLIN LEGUM

How the MPLA Won in Angola
TONY HODGES

AFRICANA PUBLISHING COMPANY
A Division of Holmes & Meier Publishers, Inc.
30 Irving Place, New York, N.Y. 10003

First published in the United States of America 1976 by
Africana Publishing Company
A division of Holmes & Meier Publishers, Inc.
30 Irving Place, New York, New York 10003

Second edition copyright © 1978 Colin Legum

Library of Congress Cataloging in Publication Data

After Angola: the war over southern Africa.

CONTENTS: Legum, C. The role of the big powers—Hodges, T. How the MPLA won in Angola.
   1. Africa, Southern—Politics and government—1975-—Addresses, essays, lectures.
   2. Africa, Southern—Foreign relations—Addresses, essays, lectures.
   3. Angola—History—Revolution, 1961-75—Addresses, essays, lectures. I. Legum, Colin. The role of the big powers. 1976. II. Hodges, Tony. How the MPLA won in Angola. 1976.
DT746.A35   1976   320.9'68'06   76-17076

ISBN 0-8419-0279-8

Printed in the United States of America

Contents

Author's Note

In a book* published in 1964 my wife and I outlined the likely course of events in southern Africa, based on what was described at the time as the 'Ben Bella strategy'. Underlying it was the straightforward military notion of knocking off the weakest enemy and moving step by step to the strongest. The first two targets, we forecast, would be Angola and Mozambique; their liberation would bring the frontiers of black Africa to the boundaries of the SA Republic, and up to the Cunene River which divides Angola from Namibia (South West Africa). 'At this point Southern Rhodesia would be held in a nutcracker. If 'White Southern Rhodesia' should try and hold out, it could be squeezed from the north, west and east. On present showing, SA would not move to protect Southern Rhodesia for the best of military and international reasons . . . The establishment of a representative government in Rhodesia would push the frontiers of black Africa up against the Limpopo in the north and the Lebombo mountains in the east. At this point the liberation movement inside SA would have the chance for the first time of establishing friendly bases all along the frontiers of the Republic . . .'

That prediction was wrong in two respects. We envisaged that Angola would crack before Mozambique, whereas the liberation struggle, in fact, was more successful in the latter territory; but since Portugal gave way in all its territories simultaneously, the argument is not affected. We were more seriously wrong in forecasting that these developments would occur by 1966-8; in the event it took six to seven years longer. Perhaps we may claim that the error over timing is less important than the analysis which successfully predicted the actual pattern of events. The reason for recalling this forecast now is not to claim any special prescience (although it is nice to be proved right), but to show how shortsighted and inaccurate Western decision-makers were in evaluating the likely course of events in that part of the world. Our views were rejected at the time by virtually everybody responsible for deciding Western policies. The fear is that, even at this critically late hour, similar errors are liable to be made again—often by the same people who were so tragically wrong before.

The aim of this small book is to present readers with a preliminary study of the role played by the major Powers in the recent struggle in Angola; to look at the implications of what happened there for the future of the violent struggle which has now begun in Rhodesia; and to argue the urgent need for a fundamental change in the mistaken Western policies in southern Africa before the situation becomes even more violent, and Western positions even less tenable. This argument is briefly set out in the first part. The following three parts are taken from the forthcoming volume of the *Africa Contemporary Record 1975-76*. Part Two is a study of the role played by the major Powers in Angola; it reaches the conclusion that the main purpose of the Russian and Cuban intervention was to undermine China's influence in Africa rather than to help the MPLA to win for its own sake, or even to weaken Western influence. Part Three is a review by Tony Hodges of the events in Angola during the critical 18 months leading up to the country's independence and the power struggle which brought military victory to the MPLA. Part Four reproduces a set of documents relevant to the Angolan struggle.

Colin Legum
LONDON. APRIL 1976.

* See Colin and Margaret Legum: *South Africa—Crisis for the West*, (Pall Mall, London; and Praeger, New York, 1964).

PART ONE

THE ROLE OF THE WESTERN POWERS IN SOUTHERN AFRICA

COLIN LEGUM

The Role of the Western Powers in Southern Africa

It is an astonishing, indeed alarming, fact that the Western nations—whether individually or collectively—are still without any policy for dealing with the now violent challenges that have begun to develop in southern Africa—a part of the world in which they cannot be thought to be without either influence or interests. Even after the considerable triumph of Russian and Cuban military intervention in Angola and the onset of a violent racial conflict in the British colony of Rhodesia—where all the weapons and military training for the black challengers are coming from the Communist countries—Britain, the US and the other NATO countries still cling—if that is not too active a word—to the carefully formulated ambiguities designed over the past 20 years to maintain a semblance of neutrality between the forces now involved in open conflict in the cockpit of southern Africa.

In the absence of a credible policy the Western nations, with their different degrees of involvement and commitment, fall back on a generally defensive posture and react on an *ad hoc* basis to each new development as it occurs. Thus Washington and London have both warned the Russians and the Cubans to keep out of Rhodesia, but without at the same time indicating what role they themselves intend to play in that struggle, and without spelling out what precisely they intend to do to stop the Russians and the Cubans if they should decide, as in Angola, not to stay out. To the Africans who, having waited patiently for a solution to the Rhodesian rebellion for 11 years, their advice is that they should be careful not to get themselves involved in a race war; and to the besieged white minority they urge 'caution and wisdom' in not getting themselves involved in a war they cannot hope to win. But these exhortations in a highly-charged emotional situation, with both sides already engaged on the battlefield, are no more than pieties. Unwilling to adopt any positive positions of their own, Western diplomacy is limited to telling others to 'behave sensibly'.

The West finds itself without any positive policy in this critical stage in the struggle over southern Africa because its traditional policies in that area have failed, and because it has not yet faced up to the necessity to formulate a choice about which side it is on, now that it is no longer credible to remain carefully neutral between the two main contenders in the conflict. So long as the white-based power system in southern Africa appeared to be under no serious threat either from their black challengers or from any major foreign Power in an area of 'traditional Western interest', it was just possible for an ambiguous policy to avoid the necessity of making a clearcut choice. While such a policy left the conflicting parties dissatisfied, it also gave each side the option of seeking to continue to try to influence Western decision-makers to back its own cause. The West was able to conduct this exercise in diplomacy by, on the one hand, registering its strong 'abhorrence' of apartheid and other racist policies while, on the other hand, refusing to take any meaningful steps either to compel change or to disengage itself from lucrative trading relations in the area generally, and from SA and Namibia in particular. As a policy, it was designed to do the least possible damage to short-term Western economic and, perhaps, strategic interests. The trouble is that it offered no long-term answer to the problems once they became acute—as was bound to happen. It was essentially a makeshift policy which postponed for as long as possible the awkward moment when a clearcut decision would have to be made.

Those who defended this policy—and they included the great majority of key

3

decision-makers in the Western capitals—believed (or pretended to believe) that 'given time' the competing forces in the region would acknowledge the realities of their situation and arrive at some realistic compromise. This policy—although it has already failed in the Portuguese colonies and Rhodesia—still governs policies towards SA, the key to the whole power structure of the region. Because Western decision-makers still don't want to upset relations too seriously with South Africa they find it more convenient to proceed in a piecemeal fashion by dealing with the remaining peripheral problems—Rhodesia and Namibia. The rationale for their attitude is that if only these peripheral problems can somehow be 'settled', without 'too much damage' and without foreign intervention, it will become easier to deal with the hard core of the crisis: SA itself. While the old policy of ambiguity might possibly have been justified on the very narrow ground of short-term Western interests so long as the conflicts had not yet become openly violent, that choice ceased to be viable once the two sides took up fighting positions and needed to know, as they now do over Rhodesia—and, increasingly, will over SA as well—what position the major Powers take in the conflict.

The anti-Western Powers of course have no difficulty in making their choice; and this has given them a clear advantage in the struggles that have already been decided in Mozambique and Angola, and which are about to be decided in Rhodesia, before moving on inexorably to Namibia and SA.

Two major changes—both of which occurred against the thrust of Western policies—showed the dramatic suddenness with which events have begun to move in southern Africa. They also indicate the startling ease with which areas accepted for centuries as Western 'salients' could be swept away, without the West either having the will or the ability to intervene actively.

The first of these changes was the sudden, but not unpredicted, collapse of Portuguese colonialism in April 1974—right against the predictions of the national Security Council of the US (*vide* Dr Kissinger's endorsement of the wrong option in the National Security Memorandum 39 of 1970), as well as of the British Foreign Office, and the NATO Defence Council evaluations of the Portuguese position in Africa. The defeat of Portuguese colonialism had three major consequences. It brought to power governments in Mozambique and Angola which had no reason to be thankful to the West and very solid reasons for being grateful to the Communist nations. It strengthened the African belief in the value of armed struggle. And it seriously undermined the old-established power-structure of the white regimes in southern Africa, leaving Rhodesia vulnerable to guerrilla attacks. SA's Prime Minister, Mr Vorster, was quick to perceive the dangers of this new situation when, in October 1974, he described the Portuguese collapse as having brought southern Africa to 'a dangerous new cross-roads'. His perceptive response to this situation was to engage in his 'exercise of diplomacy' to try and avert an armed struggle in Rhodesia and Namibia; and when this failed—largely because of the obduracy of the white Rhodesian leadership—Rhodesia's fate was left to be settled on the battlefield. The West conspicuously failed to play a meaningful part in averting the failure of the talks between the four African Presidents and SA.

The second major change was the successful intervention by the Soviet Union and Cuba in Angola which alone ensured the triumph of the Popular Liberation Movement (MPLA). The Angolan affair was important also for three reasons. First, it showed that Russia was both willing and capable of producing effective military support for an ally in a strategically crucial part of southern Africa; in doing so, the Soviets succeeded in encouraging other political movements to shift their thinking towards accepting Russian support. Second, it showed that no Western nation was willing to match the Russian involvement, so that those who had placed their reliance on the West were defeated—thus further eroding confidence in the value of Western verbal support. Finally, and perhaps most important of all, it demonstrated that it was the kiss of death for any African movement, or for any Western Power, to find itself on the same side as SA; nothing did more to legitimize the Russian/Cuban intervention in Angola than SA's intervention in the fighting. At least one lesson should be clear for Western policy-makers—that any attempt to enlist SA support in stemming a supposedly 'communist' challenge to white-ruled States is dangerously counter-productive.

However, the experience of Angola need not be taken as a sure guide to what will happen in Rhodesia. The Russians were able to play an effective role in Angola for a number of particular reasons: first, the peculiar nature of the power struggle among rival Angolan movements where there was no legally recognized government; second, SA's decision to intervene militarily; and third, the Chinese decision to opt for neutrality in the local power struggle.

Unless the South Africans decided to repeat their Angolan mistake in Rhodesia (which for the present seems highly unlikely), none of the factors which favoured the Russian role in Angola is likely to operate in Rhodesia. The Chinese are themselves actively involved in training the Zimbabwe National Liberation Army (ZNLA) and are as determined as the West to deny the Russians and Cubans any active military role. More important, none of the African Governments most directly engaged in buttressing the ZNLA offensive is willing to allow the Russians and Cubans to become directly involved in the Rhodesian struggle—other than by providing military weapons. The policy agreed among Tanzania, Zambia and Mozambique is that the Zimbabweans should liberate their own country. All three support the existing arrangements whereby the military training in the ZNLA camps should continue to be given by the Chinese as well as by the African host armies; and none favours the introduction of either Sino-Soviet rivalries or East/West rivalries in the Rhodesian struggle. The strong assumption, therefore, is that unless the South Africans become embroiled, the actual fighting will be between white and black Rhodesians alone. The hidden danger in this situation is the introduction of volunteers from SA and mercenaries from the West; if their numbers should become significant, then their presence could be perceived as a vicarious Western involvement which, again, could legitimize Cuban and other Communist involvement in the actual fighting. Of the outcome of this struggle there can be no doubt. Whether it takes two years (which is the current estimate of the planners of the ZNLA campaign) or longer, the defeat of a white minority regime in Rhodesia is inevitable. All that remains unclear is how much violence and how much bitterness there must be before majority rule is established on the battlefields of Rhodesia—and what the effects of this essentially race war will have on the situation in Namibia and SA.

The immediate outlook for Namibia will remain uncertain until SA finally makes up its mind about the kind of risks it is willing to take in granting the territory its independence by conferring black majority rule through a constitution approved by the anti-Swapo political groups in the country. Such a constitution is bound to be unacceptable to Swapo and to the OAU. How they will react it is too soon to say. Meanwhile, it is significant that the Russians appear to be putting exceptional pressures on the Swapo leadership to give up their links with their Chinese military trainers in exchange for Cuban and Russian support. That pressure is being tantalizingly applied on Swapo leaders in Brazzaville, where the Russians can demonstrate the impressive scale of military operations they established to supply MPLA with arms and in arranging for the Cuban back-up.

The portents, therefore, are clear. Well before 1980, all the territories in southern Africa, except for the Republic of SA, will have been liberated by guerrilla liberation movements, backed to the hilt by the African States and armed exclusively by

Communist countries. By then, too, SA will have begun to undergo structural changes through the 'independence' of perhaps two or more Bantustan Republics. 'Independent Bantustans' are no solution—probably the reverse—to the Republic's fundamental racial problems; but the new disintegrative forces that will be released by this balkanization of SA will certainly deepen the country's growingly serious internal contradictions. The confidence of white SA is already seriously shaken, while the morale of black South Africans is visibly rising. The Republic will come to see itself increasingly besieged from inside as well as from outside its borders; but it would be a terrible mistake to suppose that the apartheid system is bound to collapse quickly. All that can be forecast with any measure of confidence at this stage is that the Republic's internal crisis will deepen as the white minority tries to buy off the pressures of its black majority by concessions which are unlikely to yield the kind of stability which the Republic's leaders still mistakenly believe they can achieve through a policy of Separate Development.

Meanwhile, by 1980, the Russians and Chinese will have strengthened their influence in southern Africa; the African States, having seen their 'unfinished Revolution' reach the banks of the Limpopo and the spurs of the Lebombo mountains, will be in full cry for the final act of the struggle to 'liberate Africa'. The active role of the Communist nations in support of the liberation movements will have increased; and anti-Communist African leaders will find it much less easy to resist the influence of the Communists' supporters. If the Western nations should have failed to make their choice by then, their options during the last stage of the struggle will be even more sharply reduced than they have already become; their influence in southern Africa will by then have been seriously eroded, and their standing in the rest of the continent considerably weakened.

Only one question really seems to be left to Western decision-makers to decide: whether to make the choice about which side to back now, while they may still hope to influence the course of events, or later when others will be in a much stronger position to apply pressures on SA. But even postponing the choice to later no longer means 20 or 30 years; it means within the next few years.

6

PART TWO

A STUDY OF FOREIGN INTERVENTION IN ANGOLA

COLIN LEGUM

Foreign Intervention in Angola

COLIN LEGUM

'Our failure to find a solution here (in Angola) confirms that the Organization of African Unity (OAU) has no power to shape the destiny of Africa. Power is in the hands of the Super-Powers, to whom we are handing Africa by our failure.'
President Kenneth Kaunda of Zambia.[1]

That the handling of the Angolan crisis was a failure of OAU policy is as incontestable as that the Super-Powers have the 'power' in their hands: the question is why the OAU not only failed to avert the long-awaited civil war, but why it failed to uphold a cardinal principle of agreed African policy—that foreign Powers should be firmly kept out of internal African conflicts. In Angola's case, foreign Powers were deliberately invited to become participants by the country's own leaders as well as by some independent African leaders; subsequently this invitation to join in the struggle was endorsed by many of Africa's leaders—although they disagreed sharply about which type of intervention they approved.

The purpose of this essay is to attempt a preliminary evaluation[2] of the available knowledge about the way in which the Angolan conflict became internationalized, avoiding the ideological approach which has so far overshadowed discussion of the Angolan affair. The aim will be to provide an objective description of the development of the crisis from early 1975 as the basis for an evaluation of the differing pre-suppositions and claims put forward by the parties in the conflict. One area of conflicting claims raises such questions as: was the initial phase of Soviet and Cuban intervention (between March-October 1975) a reaction to American intervention in Angola—a claim made more strongly by US liberals than by the Moscow camp; or was the Russian-Cubans' massive intervention only a response to SA's military intervention as they claim; or were the Russians primarily responsible for starting the 'war of intervention', as the Chinese have insisted all the way through; or was it mainly due to the Sino-Soviet conflict in the Third World; or was Angola another stage in Russia's strategy to thrust into southern Africa, as has been claimed by Kissinger, by Vorster and by certain circles in Nato? When, in fact, did SA military forces first become actively engaged in Angola?

A second group of questions is raised by the issue of who the 'legal government' was in the country after the Portuguese left. Was it the People's Republic of Angola, proclaimed by Dr Agostinho Neto's MPLA? Or the Social Democratic Republic of Holden and Savimbi? Or was there, in fact, no legitimate authority between the time of Portugal's withdrawal on 11 November 1975 and the OAU's recognition of the MPLA Government of 22 February 1976? If there was a legitimate authority, can one properly speak of a civil war, which the Russians dispute? Or was it 'a war of intervention', which fanned the civil dispute into war as the Chinese and others claim? Finally, there are the questions raised by Africa's own role in causing the conflict to spread. Was it because of the MPLA's belief that it could achieve effective political power only through gaining military superiority? Was it the result of the policy of Zaire's President Mobutu Sese Seko in seeking to use Holden Roberto's FNLA to promote an essentially Zairean national interest? What were the separate responsibilities of FNLA and of Dr Jonas Savimbi's Unita in getting SA so heavily involved in the struggle? What was Vorster's interest in risking military intervention in Angola: was it a reaction to the Soviets' intervention; or was it an attempt by 'the imperialists' to prevent the victory of a progressive government in Luanda?

The starting-point for exploring these important questions is a brief description of Angola's political realities in the last phase of Portugal's rule.

It was no accident that, at the height of the independence crisis, each of the liberation movements should have been more or less entrenched in one of the country's three ethno-linguistic regions—Holden Roberto's FNLA among the 700,000 Bakongo of the north;[3] Jonas Savimbi's Unita among the two million Ovimbundu of the south;[4] and Agostinho Neto's MPLA among the 1.5 m Mbundu of north-central Angola (Luanda to Malanje), as well as in the major urban centres.[5] Nevertheless, although 'communal tripolarity had cleaved Angolan nationalism from its origins',[6] as a result both of the colonial experience and of the liberation struggle, simple ethnic affinities had begun to yield to modern nationalist loyalties and attitudes. Thus the provisional government of Holden Roberto and Savimbi had combined two of the ethnic regions to form a supra-tribal alternative to the MPLA government. And the MPLA itself was not simply Mbundu; it had attracted to its ranks much of the urban intelligentsia of all the communities (including mesticos and Portuguese). At one time a majority of the Portuguese were ready to give their allegiance to Unita, while the left-wing Portuguese were solidly for MPLA. The Ovimbundu themselves had, for a time, produced an internal split with a minority of support going to Daniel Chipenda,[7] an FNLA leader, and the majority to Savimbi. The FNLA could itself no longer count on the unquestioning support of the Bakongo—whose nationalism was the earliest in the country—because of their unhappy experiences at the hands of FNLA soldiers and leadership. Therefore, to describe the three rival movements as 'tribal parties' is a typical piece of over-simplification to the point of crude misrepresentation; nevertheless, it remains correct to say that each of the rivals had strong 'territorial ground' on which to base themselves during the power struggle—at first against the Portuguese and later against each other.

The period of exile and of the liberation struggle had not only failed to unite the three movements, but had made their leaders deeply mistrustful of each other—a mistrust fed by their external alliances which were based on getting support from foreign nations either in rivalry with each other (US, Russia, China) or pursuing particularist interests (Zaire).

Holden Roberto was the leader most heavily committed to an external ally—Zaire. Holden and General Mobutu Sese Seko—kinsmen through the relationships of their wives although not brothers-in-law—had developed so close a familial political relationship that even if Holden had wished to end it he could not have done so without jeopardizing his own survival, and probably his movement's as well; but it was always possible for Mobutu to discard Holden if he ever found a better way of achieving his objectives, which are discussed below. Holden also had connections with the US, China and North Korea. For a short time, during the Kennedy Administration, the CIA had supported his struggle against the Portuguese. That association (although later attacked by liberal Americans as much as by the Russians) was in fact the high point in US active opposition to Portuguese colonialism: Salazar was then still a force and Holden was at the height of his popularity in Africa although deeply unpopular in many Western circles because of the brutal killings of Portuguese families which had occurred when his forces had first launched their armed struggle in 1961. The liberals in the Kennedy Administration had failed, however, to keep the President committed to a militant, although clandestine, stand against Lisbon for longer than two years (1962-4). According to US Congress investigators it is possible that Holden may have continued to receive small payments from the CIA. What one makes of such a relationship depends entirely on one's ideology. Perhaps Holden was not the best

10

choice—but that, too, is a subjective judgement. Holden was for some years the only Angolan leader recognized by the OAU, and after an interregnum was again recognized as one of the two leaders qualifying for OAU support. The Chinese took up Holden more strongly even than the Americans, while the North Koreans gave him assistance. In Russian eyes, Holden's alliance with the Chinese and the Americans simply proves their theory of the 'imperialist alliances of the Maoists'. However, the crucial point about Holden's role in the liberation struggle is that he was committed as strongly to carrying Mobutu's flag in the area as he was to tearing down the Portuguese flag. On only one major issue did he disagree with Mobutu—over the future of the Cabinda enclave (see below).

The MPLA had no similar overriding commitments, despite its strongly Marxist leadership. Its support derived more widely than FNLA's, coming mainly from the OAU, the Soviet bloc, Cuba, Yugoslavia, China, Sweden and from the left-wing parties in Portugal. It was not until the last stage before independence that the MPLA came to depend—virtually for its survival—on Russian and Cuban help. But, by then, it had almost no other choice since the US and China were both supporting FNLA and Unita who, at that point, were challenging MPLA for power. The MPLA's own experiences with the Russians were, in fact, chequered over much of the decade preceding independence—and this applied particularly to Moscow's relations with Neto. During one of MPLA's frequent internal crises—the result of the diversity of its membership and leadership, as well as of the awkwardness of Neto's own personality—the Russians had suspended all their support to Neto's wing of the movement for almost two years (1972 and 1973), and transferred their backing to his challenger, Daniel Chipenda, who was later to join the FNLA and to play the leading role in arranging SA's military involvement in Angola. But in 1972 it had still seemed as if Chipenda's challenge for the leadership might succeed, and the Russians welcomed this prospect since they had never found it easy to deal with Neto—an introverted, secretive, touchy, cold and proud man, who tended to keep his counsels very much to himself. However, once it became clear in 1973 that the Chipenda bid was going to fail, the Russians invited Neto to Moscow where they disclosed to him that their intelligence sources in Lusaka (the temporary headquarters of MPLA) had discovered that Chipenda's men were planning to assassinate Neto. In this way the Russians could repair their broken links with Neto by doing him an immense personal service. The truth of the allegations against Chipenda was never properly established; but what is factually certain is that shortly after Neto's return from Moscow his own supporters carred out an armed attack on Chipenda and his close associates, which was frustrated only by Zambia's security forces. Neto, therefore, has reason to be grateful to Moscow for its intelligence (which Neto certainly believed to be true); but he also knows from his own experience that the Russians are capable of shifting their loyalty to suit their own particular interests. In the light of this experience it is somewhat ingenuous for Neto to have said[8] in an interview with Soviet television: 'In our relations with Socialist countries we have never felt any pressure about what policy we are to follow. For those who understand the intrigues of imperialism the conclusion is obvious.' The Russians, though, are fully justified in claiming that they had consistently supported MPLA from the start of its struggle against Portuguese colonialism. Their support was never on a large scale between 1958–75; whether it was larger than China's is not easily verifiable.

Although it is correct to describe the MPLA as a Marxist movement—in the sense that most of its leaders believe in 'scientific socialism'—it is difficult to sustain the argument that the MPLA has been either pro-Russian or pro-Communist. The vital support given to MPLA at its moment of possible defeat will undoubtedly colour the foreign orientation of the Neto government initially; yet there are good grounds to suppose that, once in power, the MPLA will show itself to be as pragmatic as Samora Machel's Frelimo in Mozambique. In his address[9] to the Afro-Asian People's Solidarity Organization conference held in Luanda in February 1976, Neto declared: 'We reaffirm our complete adherence to the policy of non-alignment. We have no intention whatsoever—nor has anyone asked it of us—of making available, or establishing, military bases in our country which are not strictly in the interests of our national defence. We have no intention of being dragged into any of the different military blocs, even though we are very much interested in the limitation of nuclear arms, and in the policy of detente aimed at establishing a climate of peace and trust among all nations of the world.' An example of MPLA's pragmatism is their dealings with the US multinational corporation, Gulf Oil, which has a lion's share of the Cabinda oil field. While the details of the exact relationship between Gulf Oil and MPLA are not yet known, what is certain is that the two parties did have secret negotiations and had an understanding between themselves. In September 1975, Gulf began paying the quarterly royalties due to Angola, worth $116 m, into the MPLA's own account, even though the country was not yet independent and MPLA was not the government; but it did control the Ministry of Finance in the Transitional Government. In December 1975, Gulf paid the next instalment into a suspense account, but only under a direct order from the US State Department to Gulf. When a British journalist wrote an article early in 1976 suggesting that MPLA was about to nationalize the Cabinda oil operations, he was promptly expelled from Luanda and his story officially denied. The MPLA has also established a direct relationship with Diamang, the powerful multinational diamond corporation (in which Harry Oppenheimer's Anglo-American Corp. has a major stake).

Alone among the liberation movements, Jonas Savimbi's Unita failed to establish any external alliances during its years of struggle, having remained largely isolated inside Angola. There was one short period when Unita made a bid to win Peking's support but this was rejected. The Chinese, in fact, gave no help to Unita until the middle of 1975—but their first shipment of arms never reached Angola. Savimbi has given this illuminating version of what had happened:[10] 'Unita, which had earlier in 1975 sent a goodwill delegation to China, used the good offices of President Julius Nyerere to help secure such armaments from China. (Nyerere, of course, after several long discussions with president Savimbi, had been duly convinced—he said at the time—of the need to support Unita, which he had by then learned was a revolutionary, Pan-African socialist party.) China agreed to help Unita in its revolutionary struggle against Soviet imperialism in Angola and in August 1975 sent Unita a vast quantity of badly needed weapons to the port of Dar es Salaam, where 15 trucks had been sent overland to pick them up for transport back to Unita bases in southern Angola. Meanwhile, MPLA-Soviet Union was on a military rampage in the south and quickly by force gobbled up Luso, Sa da Bandeira, Moçamades, Lobito and other cities where Unita has always had virtually total political support. These quick military victories, along with MPLA-Soviet bloc worldwide propaganda projecting MPLA as the "party of the people", "controlling 12 out of 16 Angolan provinces", etc, apparently convinced Nyerere that he should not—in spite of his previous agreement with China and Unita—seem to be helping Unita by allowing the use of Dar es Salaam for importation and delivery of weapons to us. When he refused to allow Unita to pick up its supplies, Nyerere offered us the spurious excuse that he did not want to further the war of brother against brother. This would have been an understandable position, except that at the very same time he was allowing the Russians and others to deliver hundreds of tons of weapons into Dar es Salaam where they were quickly flown to Luanda and other MPLA-Soviet-captured cities! In other words, it is all right and "revolutionary" for MPLA-Soviets to kill Unita militants, supporters and other Angolans; but wrong and "counter-revolutionary" for Unita to fight back in defence of the people's revolution.'

Savimbi always accepted the importance of independent Angola having close relations with both its neighbours—Zaire and Zambia. Although he finally achieved an understanding with Mobutu in 1974, the link was slender as Savimbi did not wish to become another of Zaire's satraps, and because he strongly disagreed with Mobutu's aim to achieve Cabinda's secession from Angola (see below). Zambia, with whom relations remained close since 1974, provided Savimbi with a lifeline to the outside world. At a meeting of the Presidents of Zambia, Tanzania and Botswana in April 1975 a decision was taken to support Savimbi as the leader for Angola's government of national unity. That decision was, in fact, conveyed by President Kaunda to President Ford during his official visit to Washington at the end of April. Nyerere later changed his attitude to Savimbi when he decided to back the MPLA's claim to being the legal government and his Government publicly denounced Savimbi for 'allying himself with the arch-enemy of Africa' after SA's military intervention in October 1975. Savimbi's part in the SA intervention will be discussed later. However, in March 1975, he had praised Vorster's 'responsible role' in seeking to promote detente, and had said: 'Economic co-operation with SA is only realism, however much we may be opposed to the inhumanity and injustice of apartheid.'[11] On this point he said he was willing to follow Frelimo's example in Mozambique. Savimbi also won substantial backing from the Francophone African States—especially the Ivory Coast, Senegal and Cameroon. He was promised military and other support by Nigeria and Ghana in the middle of 1975, but both later changed their policy.

All three liberation movements therefore approached independence encumbered with alliances developed either during the long years of the liberation struggle, or acquired in the short period between Portugal's decision to disengage from Africa in April 1974 and the subsequent bitter power-struggle leading up to independence in November 1976.

THE SITUATION AT THE APPROACH OF INDEPENDENCE
Portugal's hope that the Alvor Agreement signed in the Algarve on 15 January 1975[12] would result in a government of national unity had crumbled by March; and the OAU's attempt to revive these hopes through the Nakuru Agreement, reached under President Kenyatta's chairmanship on 15 June, proved equally unsuccessful under the pressures of the struggle for power between MPLA, FNLA and Unita. Nevertheless, the OAU at its summit meeting in Kampala at the end of July persisted in the increasingly hopeless task of preventing the growing violence from turning into a full-scale civil war. These efforts are described in a later section.

The Transitional Government provided for by the Alvor Agreement was established in Luanda on 28 March 1975; but it hardly survived a month because of the fighting between the MPLA and FNLA which cost 20,000 Angolan lives in the capital alone.[13] At first, Unita managed to stay out of this violent struggle: its interest was to play the role of mediator in order to establish conditions favourable to holding pre-independence elections which Savimbi, not without reason, believed he could win easily—and to which all the parties had committed themselves at Alvor.

The MPLA put the blame on FNLA for all that had gone wring after the signing of the Alvor Agreement. There is plenty of evidence that Holden, with Zaire's support, was flooding the country with arms and money ($300,000 of which came from the CIA). His arms were Chinese and Zairean, but not US since they do not supply Mobutu with weapons. Understandably suspicious of Mobutu's aims, the MPLA began to stockpile arms; these began to reach them from Russia and Yugoslavia from before March 1975. The risk of Angola's power-struggle being settled by armed force had hung heavily over the Nakuru talks in June; there was a sense of relief when Neto, Holden and Savimbi all put their signatures to a document agreeing to de-escalate the arms race in Angola and to work together. But these undertakings were to last no longer than the time it took the rivals to return hôme. Neto at once charged FNLA with ignoring the provisions of the Nakuru Agreement, while FNLA reacted by accusing MPLA (with complete justification) of seeking arms from Russia and of recruiting the former Katangese gendarmerie. Up to about May 1975 there was not yet much tangible evidence to suggest that the Russians were contemplating a major role: they were then still concentrating their efforts towards helping the Portuguese Communist Party to achieve a dominant position in the Lisbon regime. However, the Katangese gendarmerie had long been a source of Mobutu's suspicions. They were a well-trained force of between 3,500-6,000 men who had gone into exile after the defeat of their leader, Moise Tshombe, the former Katanga secessionist leader. The Portuguese colonial authorities had kept them intact as a pre-emptive threat to Mobutu in case he pushed his support for the FNLA guerrillas too far. Now the MPLA took over this old colonialist weapon with which to threaten Mobutu. Between 350-450 of the gendarmerie were killed in an engagement with the FNLA in March 1975.

In June the barely viable political situation collapsed entirely, leaving the country divided into two armed camps. Responsibility for this further deterioration—and about this there can be no reasonable doubt—belongs to MPLA, which deliberately extended the struggle between itself and what it saw as Zaire's proxy, FNLA, to include armed attacks on Unita as well. Its offices in Luanda were wrecked on 4 June and a number of its supporters killed. The attacks then spread to many parts of the country—Gabela on 10 June, Cassamba on 30 June, Henrique de Carvalho on 15 July, Kalabo on 22 July and Lukusse on 30 July. These systematic attacks could no longer be explained by MPLA as being due to mistakes by some of its 'undisciplined troops'. Finally, on 5 August, Savimbi claimed that an attempt had been made on his life when the plane in which he was travelling was fired on at Silva Porto. It is difficult, as yet, to decide the worth of this allegation, but in the suspicious atmosphere in which he was living, Savimbi saw it as a sign that 'however regretfully, Unita must declare war on MPLA and enter the fighting.'[14]

This was the beginning of an uneasy alliance between Savimbi and Holden—neither of whom trusted each other or shared each other's political attitudes. It was the end of any hope of forming a government of national unity before independence. From that point on, all three sides concentrated on winning over foreign allies willing to supply them with military and political support. All three chose to present the struggle as one of survival. and each sought to out-rival the other in bringing arms as well as foreign troops—mercenaries and volunteers—into Angola. And so the scene was set for the internationalization of what had begun as a local power struggle.

It was at this stage—July 1975—that Holden authorized Daniel Chipenda to go to Namibia for talks with the SA chief of the Bureau of State Security (BOSS) to enlist the Republic's military support. There is no evidence, either way, that Mobutu was privy to these arrangements—but it is doubtful whether Holden would have ventured on such a serious step without first getting Mobutu's approval for it.

Chipenda's mission thoroughly alarmed Savimbi, for although he was then engaged in talks about forming a joint front with Holden to stop the MPLA, they were at the same time involved in a subsidiary struggle—each trying to win the final round against each other. Savimbi was naturally concerned to defend his territorial

14

base against his fellow-Ovimbundu, Daniel Chipenda, who had been sent south to build up FNLA's support in that region.[15] If the FNLA, helped by the SA, gained a clear military advantage in the south, Savimbi's position would be seriously weakened. On the other hand, if he enlisted SA support he could have hoped to strengthen his position against FNLA and MPLA; but just when he decided on this course is not absolutely clear.

By August, the MPLA's campaign to spread its influence from the capital—from which it had earlier successfully expelled both its rivals—was largely successful. With control of 12 out of the 16 provincial capitals—and with independence less than three months off—the MPLA was in a fair way to being able to claim the right to form the legal government of independence. Of special importance in its southern advance was the fact that the MPLA forces had succeeded in capturing the key ports of Lobito, Mocamedes and Benguela; this cut off the possibility of any military supplies reaching their opponents from the sea, or from using the Benguela railway.

By the beginning of October, with less than six weeks to go before independence, Neto's forces—strongly armed by the Russians and reinforced by the first wave of Cuban support and combat troops—appeared to be heading for a military walkover. Then, suddenly, the situation changed again. On 19 October, Neto broadcast a serious warning:[16] 'The fact that the Deputy Secretary-General of the UPA*-FNLA, Daniel Chipenda, has had open contacts with certain SA groups in Windhoek, the fact that the participation of white mercenaries and Zairean military units in the invasion of the north of Angola is increasing day by day . . . the fact that Hercules C-130 aircraft and others loaded with armoured and other vehicles and armaments of various origins arrive in Angola—Negage, Bie, Huambo—daily, are proof . . . that the Angolan people and the MPLA are facing a war of aggression from international imperialism under cover of the UPA-FNLA and Unita puppet organizations . . . The Alvor and Nakuru Agreements through which the MPLA showed once again its desire to establish the basis for a peaceful transition to independence, have been betrayed in spirit and the letter by the secessionist organizations which, while pretending to be nationalist, were in fact not so, and are nothing but the conscious enemies of the independence of Angola and its people . . .'

Zaire, which had expelled the US Ambassador after an abortive coup in his army in late 1974, abruptly changed tack in September. In that month, US aid to FNLA began to flow again[17] and on 24 October the State Department asked Congress to approve an urgent $79 m military aid programme for Zaire, to be used for FNLA.

However, the real turning point in the crisis came on 23 October when SA forces entered Angola in strength as a result of the earlier negotiations with Chipenda.

By 26 October, MPLA was driven out of the key southern capital of Sa da Bandeira. Mocamedes fell two days later. Although an attempted invasion of Cabinda was halted, by the end of October the MPLA was left in control of only four of the provincial capitals. Lobito and Benguela fell to the FNLA/Unita forces (with SA help) on 3 November. By then the country was being flooded with arms. US supplies were being flown in almost daily by C-30s from Zaire and SA was putting in more troops. On the MPLA side the build-up was even more formidable. Between 1,500-3,000 Cuban infantrymen with 200 troop carriers, 50 tanks, and mobile rocket launchers arrived from Brazzaville in the Congo.[18] By September they had established a military camp at Porto Amboit, south of Luanda.

On the day before independence, the OAU Chairman, General Amin, offered to send in an African peacekeeping force. Characteristically he promised: 'During the presence of such a force in Africa, any foreign country interfering in the internal affairs of Angola will be smashed by the united Africa volunteers' forces, while

* Union of the People of Angola (UPA) was the former name of FNLA.

15

ensuring the peace in Angola until such time as the Angolans will have solved their political differences themselves and peacefully.'[19] Neto's equally characteristic reply was that: 'At this moment our country is under aggression from SA invading forces, from white mercenaries and a Zaire army . . . . This constitutes an affront to our people and a challenge to independent Africa.' He refused to have any negotiations with FNLA and Unita until they 'unequivocally and politically renounced their declaration of war.'[20] Savimbi replied: 'When elephants battle, the grass suffers. This is an old African proverb. Today in my country, rival liberation movements are at war, but a war against each other is not just a war between Angolans. Now it is the elephants who battle and we, the Angolans, still suffer, using us as their gun-bearers.'[21]

Independence Day, 11 November, dawned with the proclamation of two governments: the People's Republic of Angola formed by the MPLA in Luanda; and the Social Democratic Republic of Angola, formed by FNLA and Unita, in Huambo.

Six days later a three-pronged attack was developing against Luanda and the capital seemed threatened. Later, an MPLA spokesman disclosed that Russia and Cuba had been prepared to move in planes and tanks to Luanda; but the capital was able to defend itself with the support already in the country, and the tide once again began to turn.

Long before the Portuguese flag was hauled down on almost five centuries of colonial rule, Lisbon had abandoned all pretence of being able any longer to influence the tragic course of events. A considerable part of Portugal's half a million citizens had fled the country and relations had grown strained with all three movements, but especially with the MPLA. The final question facing Lisbon was to whom power should be legally surrendered. Replying to this question[22] at the end of October, Portugal's High Commissioner in Luanda, Admiral Leonel Cardoso, said: 'The MPLA is in control of the capital city of Angola, Luanda, and has been demanding that the legal powers be transferred to them. Portugal, however, refuses to do so, insisting that it cannot hand over power to one movement only . . . The dignity and responsibility of Portugal are at stake in this.' He added that 'there had been an initial mistake in the Portuguese policy of decolonization in Angola—that was the Portuguese ingenuousness at the time of the Alvor Agreement. Portugal really believed that the process would be carried out with the three movements working in harmony. That was the origin of the Portuguese mistake. It was stipulated in the agreement that the Portuguese forces should be limited to 24,000 men and those of the three liberation movements to 8,000 each. No supervision of this provision had been laid down, however, and each of the three movements soon had forces larger than those of the Portuguese. It then became impossible for the Portuguese forces to maintain order. Even so the Portuguese had done what they could to avoid armed confrontation and bloodshed . . . Portugal could not accept just one of the liberation movements. The Portuguese position continued to be one of neutrality, although an ever less active neutrality since the means at Portugal's disposal grew increasingly smaller. It had been argued that the MPLA has greater affinity with the spirit of the Portuguese revolution, but that was no reason to recognize just that movement. We do not have to take decisions concerning the future of the Angolan people, they must choose their own life. I only want to stress that if an order came to hand over power to only one movement, whichever it might be, I would resign. I came here with the intention of being neutral and impartial. Thus I do not admit the possibility of changing my mind tomorrow,' Admiral Cardoso said.

The Admiral did not have to go back on his word. On 3 November, Portugal's Minister of Co-operation, Admiral Victor Crespo, explained his Government's position to the OAU Chairman, General Amin in Kampala.[23] The guiding principles, he said, were set out in the Alvor Agreement, even though some of its clauses could no longer be implemented. He went on to say: 'However, the spirit of the agreement and of some of the principles laid down in it will continue to be respected by Portugal. Thus, for example, Portugal believes that Angola's territorial unity should be preserved . . . and that the Angolan nation is a single entity and must therefore be represented by a single Government administrating the Angolan State. We further believe that the organization of the Angolan Government should be achieved in Angola with the support of the friendly African countries, and in this connection we regard the OAU's present demarches as very useful. Portugal has assured the OAU Chairman that it will withdraw all its troops before 11 November . . . I further made it clear to the OAU Chairman that Portugal rejects the resort to force as a means for resolving the Angolan problem, for it believes that the solution should be sought through understanding between the Angolan political forces. I also laid much emphasis on the fact that Portugal vehemently condemns any forms of foreign interference in Angola's problems . . .'

When Admiral Cardoso lowered the flag for the last time, he made a formal statement recognizing Angolan independence but without transferring power to any of the contending governments. The OAU's position on independence day was governed by the Kampala Summit resolution[24] insisting on a government of national unity which would include all three liberation movements.

Clearly, therefore, no legal government existed in Angola at independence—only two rival claimants. The issue of 'legality' was still to be fought over—with weapons and through each side's ability to attract international diplomatic recognition.

The MPLA had a clear advantage over its rivals in that its supporters were keen to recognize it and to help its claims to legality. About 30 States granted it immediate recognition, led by the Soviet bloc countries, but including fewer than one-third of the OAU's members who included the four former Portuguese colonies, Congo, Guinea and Algeria. The majority of OAU members still stuck to their line of not recognizing either of the claimants. This put the FNLA/Unita government at a strong disadvantage, which was thoroughly exploited by the MPLA and its supporters.

THE ROLE OF THE SOVIET UNION

Russia was the only major Power which refused to abide by OAU decisions that neither of the claimants should be recognized.[25] It openly challenged the African stand by addressing two communications[26] to the OAU Chairman, General Idi Amin, saying that it 'cannot be unconcerned over the developments in Angola', and asking that Uganda should recognize the MPLA Government—a request which, perhaps, it felt could be made with some confidence because Russian arms had become indispensable to Amin's army. But the Russians had miscalculated Amin's own African commitments. He condemned the Soviet Union for its arrogance in arbitrarily demanding that Uganda follow Moscow's dictate by supporting one of the liberation movements. As a sovereign country, he said, Uganda refused to be dictated to; it stood by the OAU's policy of recognizing all three liberation movements. The Soviet Union had no right to interfere in African affairs, and he censured it for interfering in Uganda's own afairs. He went on to criticize the 'arrogance' of the 'vodka-drinking' Russian Ambassador in Kampala, and demanded his recall. This led to a diplomatic rupture between the two countries which, however, lasted for only six days—a sign of the mutual interests of both countries. Amin continued to argue that 'the MPLA does not represent the majority of the Angolan people,[27] while the Russians insisted that 'it was clear for everyone that the MPLA, which had the support of the majority of the population in the country and the new Government in Portugal and the progressive public of the whole world, was capable of making a most decisive contribution for preparing the country for the proclamation of independence scheduled for 11 November and also to become the guiding force of Angolan society.'

The basis of Russian policy is that it is assisting 'Angola's legitimate government based on the internationalist principle of supporting the nations' struggle for freedom and independence'.[28] Although Moscow had originally favoured 'a transitional Government with the participation of representatives of various movements', it claimed that affairs in Angola had taken a different turn for which 'the blame lies with the leaders of the secessionist alignments which unleashed an armed struggle with active support from outside.'[29] Moscow insisted that there could be 'no talk whatever of civil war in Angola: foreign military intervention is being carried out against the lawful government of the young republic, with a section of deluded Angolans who are under the influence of splitter groups, being used as a cover.'[30] This theme of 'splitters' or 'splittists' recurs in every Soviet analysis of the Angolan situation. The presupposition on which Russia bases its case is that MPLA is the authentic nationalist movement who 'started an uprising in Luanda on 4 February 1961[31] and that the 'Portuguese helped Holden Roberto to set up his own armed forces to fight the genuine patriots, and these forces struck at the MPLA.'[32]

The historical fact, of course, is that the MPLA began its urban nationalist resistance much earlier—in 1958—whereas the modern phase of the armed struggle was started by FNLA in 1961. Since its original attack led to the brutal killings of hundreds of Portuguese settlers, it hardly fits the allegation that the Lisbon regime was behind Holden. The Russians charge Holden with being 'a big businessman, the owner of gambling houses and taxi-cab companies in Zaire . . . and that he has been on the CIA payroll for 15 years . . .'[33] It correctly describes his role in relation to Mobutu's aims.

Russia's defence of its own policies is convincing when it compares its support for MPLA with the US role. 'Where,' it asks,[34] 'were the "friends of the Angolan people in all those long years while the Angolans fought their foreign oppressors?" ' They accuse the US of engaging in a 'military intervention . . . with their junior partners, the racist regime in the Republic of SA . . . to defend the general interests of imperialism, the profits of an individual monopoly . . .'—i.e. Gulf Oil.

This Marxist analysis of the US involvement being dictated by economic interests does not explain a basic contradiction: since the MPLA firmly controls Cabinda (the area of Gulf's operations) it would have suited US interests better had Washington backed the MPLA—an argument strengthened by the fact that Gulf (as already mentioned) had begun to make its terms with the MPLA and was, in fact, strongly opposed to the State Department's policy of preventing it from continuing to make its oil royalty payments to MPLA. So far as the Gulf 'monopoly interest' was concerned, its best interest was for the US to recognize MPLA.

Moscow's attitude to the criticism that its Angolan policy threatens East/West detente are: 'False . . . they distort the nature of events in Angola and the essence of international detente . . . Detente does not mean freedom of action for reactionaries and aggressors of every stripe . . .'[35] And again:[36] 'Sometimes, for instance in Angola, sharp conflict situations arise which are caused by the fact that colonialism and forces supporting it do not want to quit the historical arena . . . And such a liberation struggle is taking place in Angola now. Is it perhaps opposed to the aims of detente? Of course not.' And the Russian reply[37] to Western criticism of Russian 'intervention' is that 'the neo-colonialists and racists would like to keep a bastion in southern Africa to confront all the progressive countries on the African continent.

It is no secret that military, strategic and economic interests play a considerable role in this'. The same report suggests that 'in Washington, too, they admit that the troops of the SA regime were introduced into Angola with the knowledge of the US and at the direct request of Unita'.

In sum, therefore, the Russian case is that what is happening in Angola is not a 'civil war' but 'an overt imperialist aggression against the sovereign People's Republic of Angola. It is a struggle by its people against gross interference in its internal affairs'. This, of course, is precisely the charge levelled by Amin against the Russians for helping one of the parties in the conflict to achieve their military supremacy. For perfectly understandable reasons the Russians are, in fact, keen to acknowledge their role in helping the MPLA to victory:[38] 'It can be said now that, thanks to the staunchness of the MPLA fighters and the assistance from the socialist countries, the aggressor's plans to eliminate the People's Republic of Angola by *blitzkrieg* methods have been thwarted, but the aggression, far from being stopped, is becoming more overt and assuming an increasingly wide scale.'

Russian attacks on the US have throughout been much less harsh than on the Chinese.[39] 'The Peking leadership is playing a shameful role in the struggle against the national liberation movement of the Angolan people. Peking is supplying countries neighbouring with Angola with large consignments of arms which the splitters are using to fight the democratic forces of Angola and is sending military instructors and specialists and training military personnel for the traitors to the Angolan people. One of the splitters' leaders, Holden Roberto, openly declared that all his men have been trained by the Chinese and, what is more, the Chinese were giving him unconditional aid (sic). Not only do the Maoists themselves interfere in the affairs of independent Angola, but they are taking joint action with the imperialists and are cynically trying to justify the practical actions of the racialist regime in SA.'

The role of Sino-Soviet rivalry in Angola is discussed below.

Russia's military involvement in Angola divides into three phases—the period of the liberation struggle (1958-74); the period between Portugal's announcement that it would surrender power and the SA intervention (April 1974-October 1975); and the period leading up to and immediately beyond independence (October 1975-March 1976). The two latter sets of dates are particularly relevant to the argument that Soviet intervention came in response to US military aid and to the Russian claim that their military intervention was mainly concerned with stopping the SA 'invasion'.

There can be no reliable figures of the amount of Russian aid given to MPLA during the first period; one source,[40] based on Western intelligence guestimates, puts the figure at £27 m from 1960-74. For the second period—April to October 1975—official US estimates put Russian shipments to Angola (excluding the Cuban involvement which is considered separately) at 27 shiploads of military equipment and 30-40 air supply missions flown in AN-22 cargo planes. The same sources put the number of Soviet military advisers in Angola at 170-200. The precise number of shipments is less important for the purpose of this analysis than the timing of the shipments and the kind of arms supplied. Dr Neto confirmed[41] in a radio interview at the end of January 1976 that the Russians had supplied him with MiG 21s, T34 and 54 tanks, APCs, anti-tank and Sam-7 missiles, rocket launchers and AK-47 automatic rifles. While denying that the USSR had also sent military advisers, he added: 'Such advisers were only in Congo-Brazzaville, and from there they have tried to help the MPLA.'

The first definite evidence[42] of sizeable Russian and Yugoslav arms reaching Angola goes back to 25 March 1975 when 30 Russian cargo planes arrived in Brazzaville—the staging post for Russian and Cuban military shipments to Angola.

In April, c. 100 tons of arms arrived by air in Dar es Salaam for transhipment. In April, a Greek-registered ship left Dar es Salaam with military supplies for MPLA. In the same month a Yugoslav freighter was turned away from Luanda by the Portuguese and off-loaded its cargo at Pointe-Noire, the port for Brazzaville. At least one other Yugoslav ship and one Russian ship also unloaded arms at Pointe-Noire in April. In July, the *Sun Rise,* a Cypriot ship, off-loaded its supplies in Luanda.[43] All this is sufficient evidence to show that a steady flow of Russian arms (as distinct from Cuban supplies) had begun to reach the MPLA during the first half of 1974.

This flow became a flood from the middle of October, shortly before SA had entered the arena on the 23rd of that month. By November the military weapons in Angola were sufficient to turn the tide of battle which had flowed against MPLA after SA's intervention. A number of correspondents[44] reported on the impact made by the sophisticated communist weapons on the battles fought after November 1975. The Russians proudly admit (see above) that their contribution was decisive in averting a *blitzkrieg* from succeeding against MPLA.

Although there has been a number of reports about Russian military advisers in Luanda—ranging from 200–400—the only hard piece of evidence is that Igor Ivanovich Uvarov, a *Tass* 'correspondent', who is a leading member of the Soviet military intelligence, GRU, was active in the capital.[45]

By the middle of January, according to Dr Kissinger, Russian military aid had reached $200 m.

THE ROLE OF CUBA

Cuba's interest in Angola goes back a long way—to the early 1960s when Guido Sanchez first arrived in Nkrumah's Ghana to make contacts with the anti-Portuguese colonial leaders in exile there. He had a diplomatic post in London. The Cuban 'revolutionary connection' is explained by Castro and the late Che Guevara's early interest in promoting revolution in Latin America, which brought them into contact with the left-wing opposition in Brazil, and as a direct consequence with Portuguese-speaking revolutionaries. Havana was particularly interested in the martyr-hero of Guinea-Bissau, Amilcar Cabral—although Cabral's ideas about armed struggle were different from Guevara's. Cuban commandos were first sent to Africa to assist Cabral's PAIGC. The Cubans also had a military training team in the Congo People's Republic, at one time the headquarters of the MPLA. Once the Russians had decided to embark on a major involvement in Angola—without 'a single Russian soldier being involved' (a regular theme in Soviet disclaimers about their actual role in the territory)—it was obvious that they should enlist the voluntary support of Castro; and it was equally obvious why the great majority of Cubans sent to Angola were black.[46]

The Cuban intervention in Angola was initially clandestine—the first mention of it to the Cuban people was made at the end of January 1976, more than six months after the troops had left home. Fidel Castro has explained his country's intervention on two grounds—'to prevent the invasion by SA, and as a moral duty.'[47] Cuba's delegate to the Afro-Asian People's Solidarity Organization conference in Luanda, Sr Peralta, claimed that the first Cuban combat units had arrived on 5 November 1975, 'only after the SA invasion'.[48] And Castro told a Press conference that Cuban combat troops went into action because 'on 23 October the panzer columns of SA launched an invasion into Angola in a German *blitzkrieg* style of war.'[49]

The Cubans, like the Russians, insist that they were not involved in any serious way in Angola before the SA invasion. What evidence is there to the contrary? One Cuban, taken prisoner by FNLA, gave details of his unit's arrival from Brazzaville in August 1975, almost two months before the SA arrival.[50] FNLA sources say 50

Cubans arrived in Brazzaville on 25 July to assist in handling Russian arms. The first Cubans actually seen in operation—by Unita's commanders—appeared during the fighting that led to the capture of Lobito by MPLA in the middle of August.

There is little doubt that the Cubans were first brought into Brazzaville before July 1975 and it is feasible, therefore, that Cuban combat troops were later drafted in batches to Angola—their numbers increasing dramatically from the first unofficial US estimates of 1,500 to 3,000 (in the middle of November) to the estimate of 12,000 in the first week of February 1976. (Other estimates of their strength vary from between 5,000 and 12,000. The total Cuban armed forces number 90,000.) The mobilization and transport of such large numbers, both by air and by sea, would require at least six weeks from the time the decision was taken; so it is reasonable to assume that the Moscow-Havana agreement was taken at least in May 1975. The evidence of the Cubans having spearheaded the fighting of the MPLA troops is overwhelming; this is hardly surprising in view of the sophisticated weapons that were used and which few MPLA troops had been trained to handle. Making allowance for the Havana focus of the struggle in Angola, there is considerable justification for Castro's claim that 'if it had not been for Cuba's assistance, SA would have swallowed up Angola.'[51]

THE ROLE OF CHINA

Like Russia, China supported the Angolan liberation movement from the start of the struggle; unlike Russia, however, the Chinese accepted the OAU's decision at the Kampala Summit that support should go to all three movements.[52] The Chinese military experts, who had been training FNLA units in their camps in Zaire, left almost three weeks before independence. In a farewell speech, the military group's leader, Li Tung, said that unity between Zaireans, Angolans and Chinese would be 'eternal despite the distance separating them'. He added that the Angolans would 'conquer in their struggle against the hegemony of the Super-Powers.'[53]

The Russians alleged, however, that the Chinese withdrawal was only a screen for them to continue their support for FNLA clandestinely through large shipments of arms.

Some reports[54] suggest that the gap left in the FNLA camps by the Chinese withdrawal was partly filled by North Korean instructors who were already in Zaire as part of a military training programme for Mobutu's army. But there is no hard evidence of this.

From 1958, Peking's only link with Angola was through the MPLA which it never stopped supporting, although no military aid appears to have been sent after the end of 1974. The Chinese have never criticized the MPLA. They explain their policy of ‚supporting all three movements' as meaning that if they cannot get weapons to all three sides, none should go to any single movement.

Although Unita tried to enlist Chinese support in the early 1970s by adopting a Maoist programme at one of their conferences in the bush,[55] their appeal was ignored until early 1975, when the Chinese sent their first shipment of arms to Savimbi through Tanzania; but, as described earlier, this consignment in fact never arrived.

Peking's involvement with FNLA began in 1973—the year Mobutu repaired his damaged relations with China; it was also a time of low military activity in Angola due largely to the internal power-struggle in the MPLA between Neto, Chipenda and Joaquim Pinto de Andrade.[56] With Frelimo pressures building up, the Portuguese had been able to switch troops from Angola to Mozambique. Faced with this situation, Nyerere and Kaunda were receptive to proposals from Mobutu that the OAU should stop supporting the MPLA alone and make more help available to

FNLA and enable it to strengthen its role. Since Chinese military instructors were already training Frelimo troops in Tanzania, it was natural to turn to them to complement the Zairean army trainers in the FNLA camps. When Nyerere put this proposal to the Chinese, they readily fell in with the plan. Meanwhile, Holden had followed up Mobutu's visit to Peking and was promised a team of 250 military instructors. The first group arrived in the latter part of 1973.[57]

The consequence of China's support for FNLA was a cooling off in the relations between MPLA and Peking and the development of closer ties with Moscow—especially after the Russians had changed their policy back to support for Neto. Peking's attitude to the Angolan situation was summed up in a statement issued on the day of Angolan independence:[58]

'The Chinese Government and people extend their warm congratulations on this victory to the Angolan people and all the three Angolan liberation organizations. But it has not been possible to form a government of national unity, and an unfortunate situation of division and civil war has appeared in Angola after independence. This is entirely the result of the rivalry between the two Super-Powers, and particularly the undisguised expansion and crude interference of the Soviet Union. Differences among the three Angolan liberation organizations were something normal and could have been reconciled by them through peaceful consultations under the banner of national unity free from outside interference. But the Soviet leadership brazenly disregarded the various agreements concluded among the three Angolan liberation organizations under the encouragement of the OAU on strengthening unity and achieving independence on a joint basis. They deliberately created a split among the liberation organizations, sent in large quantities of arms, supported one organization alone and wantonly slandered and attacked the other two organizations, and thus single-handedly provoked the civil war in Angola. The Soviet Union has also tried constantly to sow discord and create disharmony among African States. These actions of the Soviet leadership have fully revealed its true features as social-imperialism. Many leaders of African States, and OAU in particular, have made tremendous efforts of mediation to help the three Angolan liberation organizations make up their differences and put forward a series of positive suggestions for the three organizations immediately to stop the civil war and establish a government of national unity. This just stand of the OAU is in full conformity with the interests of the people of Angola and all Africa. It is highly appreciated and resolutely supported by the Chinese Government. The Chinese Government and people have always deeply sympathized with and firmly supported the Angolan people in their just struggle for national independence against Portuguese colonialism and sincerely hope that the three Angolan liberation organizations, setting store by the interests of the Angolan nation and the whole situation, will unite themselves, remove their differences, oppose the common enemies, expel Super-Power meddling and interference and work together to establish a united, unified and truly independent Angola with national concord.'

SINO-SOVIET RIVALRY IN ANGOLA

The animosity between China and Russia over Angola exceeded anything either might have felt about US and other Western intervention. For the Third World it was a stunning experience of the bitterness of Sino-Soviet rivalry; but for Africa, especially, it came as a revelation which resulted in the beginning of a reassessment of their attitudes to both world communist centres. While the Chinese followed their usual soft style of diplomacy—explaining their position firmly but without making any demands or threats—the Russians adopted a more bluntly hectoring tone towards African Governments. They openly flaunted the OAU position when it went against them at the Kampala Summit in July 1975, and they approved of it when it moved closer to their own position after the Addis Ababa Summit in February 1976. Their peremptory demand that Uganda should recognize MPLA shows the toughness of Russian diplomacy when they.become committed to particular goals. They also came into open conflict with Zaire and with Zambia—whose President was moved to warn against the danger of 'the tiger and its cubs' in Africa (see below). And they strongly criticized[59] Egypt for its 'strange attitude' in keeping silent when 'Cairo understands better than anyone the significance of public solidarity at the grave hour of imperialist aggression . . . Can the Egyptian people forget the noble positions taken up by African countries who severed diplomatic relations with Israel out of solidarity with Egypt . . .' This particular criticism simply ignored the division of attitudes among the African countries themselves.

However, after SA's intervention, Russia's toughly aggressive policy may be thought to have been correct in retrospect and may have strengthened its position, (especially in southern Africa), and even though African leaders did not necessarily approve of the Russian methods.

It still remains unclear how much damage was done to China's influence in Africa as a result of the MPLA's military victory achieved largely through Soviet-Cuban aid. African countries whose links have been closer with China than with the Soviets—especially Tanzania and Mozambique—were awkwardly placed when they found the Russians on their side and the Chinese against them.

Russia and China both used Angola to justify their allegations that the other was intent on world domination. Thus, Moscow spoke of Peking's false doctrine about the role of the two Super-Powers as 'a cunning trick of the Maoists who dream of dominating the world'.[60] In a condemnation of the Chinese role in Angola, Moscow proclaimed:[61] 'The present leadership of the PRC are taking considerable pains in order to justify the so-called vanguard role of China in the world revolutionary process and represent it as one of the truest and most consistent allies of the Afro-Asian and Latin American peoples in their struggle for national liberation, against imperialism, colonialism and neo-colonialism. But events have proved absolutely false the Maoists' representation of Peking as a factor working to cement the national-liberation forces of Angola, a factor preventing a split between them. Quite the reverse, all action taken by the Peking leadership shows that the Maoists, who are seeking their own hegemonic goals, have not stopped subversive activity against the Angolan people for a single minute, that they gave active support to pro-imperialist groupings and organizations, pushing them to take action against the genuine representatives and vanguard of the Angolan people—the MPLA.'

The Chinese counter-attacked[62] by claiming that what the Russians had done in Angola 'fully revealed their ferocious features as social-imperialists', adding: 'People have become increasingly aware that in contending for hegemony with the other Super-Power, the Soviet revisionists stoop to anything to frenziedly penetrate and expand in Africa in a vain attempt to replace old colonialism. Their interference in the internal affairs of Angola constitutes an important step in their scramble for hegemony in Africa, the aim being to place strategically important Angola which is rich in natural resources in their neo-colonialist spheres of influence. But the Soviet revisionists will never succeed in their sinister design.'

Peking accused the Soviets of 'starting the war in Angola',[63] a view they sought to justify by accusing the Soviets of having 'deliberately created a split among the liberation organizations, sent in large quantities of arms, supported one organization alone, and wantonly slandered and attacked the other two organizations—and thus single-handedly provoked the civil war in Angola.'[64]

Against this Chinese version of what had happened, the Russians put much of the blame on Peking:[65] 'The Maoists sent weapons, money and military instructors to Angola. They sent them not to the legal Government recognized by many countries in Africa, Asia and other continents, but to those separatist elements which embarked on an armed struggle against the Government. Moreover, for the umpteenth time, Peking turned out to be in the same camp as the open enemies of the national liberation movement: the Portuguese facists, the SA racists, and the agents of international monopolies which nurture neo-colonialist plans. And, if there is now a threat of civil war in some regions of Angola, if shots have been fired there and innocent blood has been spilt, then considerable responsibility for this is borne by the Peking hegemonists, who have again done a deal with the most infamous international reactionary elements. Angolans are killed in their own land by Chinese arms. Peking will not succeed in concealing this fact with distracting manoeuvres of any kind.'

In all these exchanges of unpleasantries, neither Peking nor Moscow spent much time in criticizing the Western role in Angola—although both vehemently attacked SA's military intervention. The Russians, on a few occasions, suggested that the SA attack had been carried out with the foreknowledge of the US[66] and they repeatedly alleged that the Chinese had placed themselves in the same camp as the SA racists and other Western imperialists.[67]

What is especially striking is the way both Moscow and Peking used the Angolan affair to seek to influence Third World countries against each other. The Russians even tried to influence Chinese opinion against their own leadership. A Moscow broadcast in Chinese[68] illustrates the Russian campaign to win over friends in the Third World: 'People in Africa who follow the political stratagems of the Peking leadership are not, of course, surprised at the Mao Tsetung regime's present attitude, which stops at nothing to undermine the militant alliance between the countries of the socialist community and the African national liberation movements. Peking has long ago placed its hopes on renegades who serve the interests of imperialism. Mao Tsetung and his ilk certainly know that the FNLA and Unita claim that they are specific examples of the national liberation cause of the Angolan people—affirming that they have substantial connections with neo-colonialists. It suffices to point out that the leaders of those groups are former secret policemen notorious for their many crimes committed on behalf of Portugal . . . [Allegations against Holden Roberto.] According to reports, these groups also enjoy tremendous assistance from the CIA. On many occasions the so-called revolutionaries in Peking have sided with the ferocious enemy of the African people. This Roberto whom we have just mentioned boasted not long ago: "All my troops are equipped and trained by the Chinese." This helps us to conclude that there is a world of difference between Mao Tsetung's words and deeds. The Angola issue is evidence that, although Chungnanhai claims it supports people striving for their freedom and independence, it actually shamelessly betrays the interests of African countries and people.'

Peking reproached the Soviet 'arch criminal' with having supplied one side of the Angolans with arms of destruction and of then resorting to the trick of a thief crying 'stop thief'.[69] 'With a view to sowing discord, confusing public opinion and shifting the blame on others, they blatantly slandered China and some African countries for "interfering in the Angolan people's internal affairs." But who will be deceived by their despicable and clumsy tactics?'[70]

The Afro-Asian People Solidarity Organization (AAPSO), which plays an important role in supporting Moscow's policies against Peking in the Third World, staged an international rally in Luanda in January 1976. Its purpose was explicitly stated[71] by one of its leading officials, Aleksandr Dzasokhov, the deputy-chairman of the Soviet Afro-Asian Solidarity Committee: 'Developments in Angola reveal the unsavoury role of the Maoist leadership which seeks to wreck the process of decolonization in that African country. The political line of Maoism in Angola, continuing Peking's general course for wresting the national liberation movement from the other revolutionary forces of our time—the countries of the socialist community—once again confirms the hegemonistic designs *vis-à-vis* the Afro-Asian peoples. . . . In the struggle against the national liberation movement in Angola, the present leadership of the PRC factually entered into a collusion with the US, the racialists from the Republic of SA and the imperialist placemen.'

THE ROLE OF THE UNITED STATES

US policy in Angola was inhibited by two major weaknesses: its role during the anti-Portuguese colonial struggle which had ended leaving Washington on the losing side; and the refusal by a Congress, wrestling with the aftermath of Vietnam, Watergate and CIA exposure, to support the Administration's policy proposals on Angola.[72] American liberals saw Angola as 'a distant event'[73] in which the US should not become involved. Their view coincided with that of conservatives who wanted no new foreign adventures. 'Angola does not mean a damn thing to the future of this country,' was the comment of one Democratic Congressman, John Burton.[74] The coalition of forces was strong enough to block any serious proposals coming from President Ford's Administration. Throughout the US debate there was a preoccupation with American domestic interests and virtually no serious discussions about any of the serious questions of principle raised by the Angolan affair.[75]

Ford and Kissinger shared the widespread American wish to keep out of the Angolan struggle. According to Kissinger:[76] 'The US policy until well into the summer was to stay out of Angola—to let the various factions work out their own arrangements between themselves. We accepted in Mozambique without any difficulty a pro-Marxist faction that came to power by indigenous means, or perhaps with some minimum outside support in the Frelimo.'

Why, then, did the US become involved at all? Partly because of serious miscalculations and mistakes by successive Administrations. The Kennedy Administration, as has already been mentioned, had briefly supported Holden Roberto on a limited scale; but the dominant US policy was based on a need not to oppose Portugal openly for Nato and other security interests. Under the Nixon and Ford Administrations, largely because of Kissinger having misread the situation in southern Africa and having dismissed the likelihood of the anti-Portuguese liberation movements winning,[77] American policy was, in fact, hostile to MPLA, FNLA and Unita. The Portuguese collapse in April 1974 also saw the collapse of US policy in that area. The US in fact had only two major interests to defend—that of Gulf Oil (see above) and to deny anti-Western Powers a strong foothold in southern Africa. As Kissinger pointed out, it did not matter whether a Marxist government took power, as in Mozambique, but whether Russia acquired a major role in independent Angola. However, there was one complicating factor which upset Kissinger's policy towards Angola—the American interest in Zaire, an outflow from the earlier Congo crisis. Although Mobutu's relations with Washington were never easy—he had twice expelled US Ambassadors—he was always ready to call on the US for assistance whenever he was in serious difficulties. It was Mobutu's distress signal early in 1975—after an abortive coup in his army, and with the situation in Angola developing in a way he felt to be a threat to his position—that led Kissinger to take the first major step towards getting the US involved in Angola. In mid-July 1975 he requested Congress to vote a $79 m emergency aid programme for Zaire, mainly intended to provide arms for FNLA.[78]

Kissinger's critics argue that it was this act which started the arms race with the Russians—their presupposition being that Moscow would not otherwise have become involved or, at least, not as heavily as it did. This argument ignores entirely the Sino-Soviet aspect of Russia's involvement. The first US supply of money aid ($300,000), not of arms, to FNLA was made early in 1975; but by March the Russians had already begun their policy of escalating their arms' shipments, over and above the arms they had been delivering throughout the liberation struggles; and from the middle of the year the Cubans were already deeply involved. The first US arms arrived in September 1975.

Even before March 1975, on at least two occasions Kissinger had suggested to Moscow that both Super-Powers should stay out of Angola in the interests of detente. The Russian answer was to accelerate their arms' flow. As already stated, they repudiated the idea that detente either precluded their helping MPLA or that their role in Angola need set back the cause of detente. Whether Russia would have embarked on this course if Congress had not openly shown its willingness to allow the US to play a counter-vailing role remains a matter for speculation.

By the middle of 1975 the US was faced with a serious decision: whether to halt its support for FNLA and Unita by making a unilateral decision (as the Chinese had done), or whether to increase its aid. The State Department was itself divided over what should be done, with the head of the Africa Bureau, Nathaniel Davies, (who had been hand-picked for the job by Kissinger[79]) so strongly opposed that he was relieved of his post in September.[80] The CIA, too, was opposed to a larger US military programme being funnelled through Zaire.[81] More important, both Houses of Congress were overwhelmingly opposed. (Marxist analysis, which assumes a monolithic US imperialist commitment to defend its monopoly of financial interests, does not deal with this phenomenon.) Only Ford and Kissinger remained determined to see the US assume a larger role in Angola—a decision strengthened by the size of Cuba's involvement. But even the emotive issue of the Cuban presence failed to provoke a reaction sympathetic to the Administration's wishes.

Arguing his case before the Senate, Kissinger said on 29 January 1976 that the 'outcome in Angola will have repercussions throughout Africa'. The confidence of neighbouring countries, like Zambia and Zaire, would be severely shaken, he said, 'if they see that the Soviet Union and Cuba are unopposed in tneir attempt to impose a regime of their own choice in Angola'. He defended his policy favouring a clandestine role on these grounds: 'We chose covert means because we wanted to keep our visibility to a minimum; we wanted the greatest possible opportunity for an African solution. We felt that overt assistance would elaborate a formal doctrine justifying Great Power intervention—aside from the technical issues such as in what budgetary category this aid should be given, and how it could be reconciled with legislative restrictions against the transfer of US arms by recipients. The Angolan situation is of a type in which diplomacy without leverage is impotent, yet direct military confrontation would involve unnecessary risks. Thus it is precisely one of those grey areas where covert methods are crucial if we are to have any prospect of influencing certain events of potentially global importance.'

President Ford took an even more severe approach in a letter he addressed to the House of Representatives on 27 January 1976. 'This imposition of a military solution in Angola will have the most profound long-range significance for the US. The US cannot accept as a principle of international conduct that Cuban troops and Soviet arms can be used for a blatant intervention in local conflicts, in areas thousands of miles from Cuba and the Soviet Union, and where neither can claim an historic national interest. If we do so, we will send a message of irresolution not only to the leaders of African nations but to US allies and friends throughout the world.' By an overwhelming vote of 323 to 99, the House of Representatives rejected the President's appeal. He accused them of having 'lost their guts'.

Three days before the US moved towards accepting the victory of the Russian/Cuban-backed MPLA, Kissinger spoke of the possible consequences of what had happened in Angola for the future of international relations.[82] 'When one Great Power tips the balance of forces decisively in a local conflict through its military intervention—and meets no resistance—an ominous precedent is set, of grave consequence even if the intervention occurs in a seemingly remote area. Such a precedent cannot be tolerated if a lasting easing of tensions is to be achieved and, if the pattern is not broken now, we will face harder choices and higher costs in the future.'

On 6 February, Senator Dick Clark, chairman of the Senate sub-committee on Africa, proposed that the US should begin negotiations with the MPLA acknowledging that 'the tide of history' was on their side. This particular American verdict was a much more confident one than that given by many of Africa's leaders.

US military aid to FNLA and Unita, since January 1975, was of the order of $31 m. However, the Select Committee of Intelligence of the US House of Representatives suggested it might have been higher because of the use of secret CIA funds. Up to June 1975 the committee found that only c. $6 m worth of military supplies had been shipped to FNLA: this had risen sharply to c. $31 m by November 1975—after the escalation of Russian and Cuban supplies and commandos. There is an unexplained discrepancy between the committee's claim that some arms had been shipped by June and the Administration's insistence that the first US arms—as opposed to funds—only arrived in September.

THE ROLE OF WESTERN EUROPE

The European countries played a comparatively insignificant role in the Angolan struggle. Most countries, including Britain, chose to remain neutral as between the rivals, although strongly hostile to the Russian, Cuban and SA intervention. Sweden was alone in openly supporting MPLA. There was some concern in Nato about a possible threat to Western shipping if the Russians were given military facilities in Angola. Nato's Secretary-General, Dr Joseph Luns, criticized the US Congress for cutting off the flow of military assistance to the anti-MPLA forces. 'The consequences', he thought, 'might be rather serious.'[83] However, when Kissinger warned Nato in December 1975 of the dangers he foresaw in Angola he found a general unwillingness on the part of his allies to make up for the reluctance of his own Congress by providing weapons to FNLA and Unita.[84]

The French role still remains obscure. There were reports when President Giscard d'Estaing visited Zaire early in 1975 that he had given support to Mobutu's policy of getting Cabinda separated from Angola. The French role was 'vigorously condemned' by the MPLA Minister of Interior who accused 'French capitalist groups' of conspiring with Americans to divide Cabinda.[85] A report in *Le Monde* (3 September 1975) that France had delivered arms to the FNLA was promptly denied by the French Defence Ministry. After the MPLA's military victory, the French Government was so quick off the mark to recognize Dr Neto's Government that it risked offending its EEC associates by making its announcement ahead of the time scheduled for a collective West European recognition.

Portugal, whose relations with MPLA had deteriorated since 1974—especially after the defeat of the Communist elements in the Lisbon Government—nevertheless strove hard to maintain a careful neutrality during the last difficult phase of its withdrawal.[86] But it was slow to recognize the MPLA, both because of the thorny economic questions which remain to be settled and because of strong anti-MPLA feelings among the 800,000 or so Portuguese who had fled Angola.

THE ROLE OF MERCENARIES

Mercenaries played a major role in the Angolan struggle. The only 'hired gunmen' on the side of MPLA were the 3,500 to 6,000 Katangese gendarmerie (see earlier) who, collectively, greatly outnumbered the 1,200 or so Portuguese, British, French, Greek, SA and American mercenaries who fought with FNLA and Unita. However, these mercenaries were specially picked for their professional skills. Neither Holden Roberto nor Savimbi ever denied that they had recruited mercenaries, although they claimed in their defence that they were necessary to offset the 'Cuban, Russian and Katangese mercenaries' fighting with MPLA. The numbers of mercenaries on the anti-MPLA side rose swiftly in late January 1976 after the SA army had begun to withdraw to the southern border; but this rapidly recruited force turned out to be an expensive folly—paid for out of CIA funds.[87]

THE ROLE OF THE OAU

Although the African Governments were divided over who to support in Angola, the OAU was able to maintain a broad concensus on four aspects of its Angolan policy until SA's intervention in late October 1975: support for the idea of a Government of National Unity; acceptance of MPLA, FNLA and Unita as genuine nationalist movements entitled to a place in such a government; the need to maintain the country's geographical integrity, including Cabinda; and opposition to any type of external intervention.[88] These views were endorsed once again at the OAU Summit at Kampala at the end of July 1975, when General Idi Amin became current Chairman.

Amin's idiosyncratic role as Chairman was an important contributory factor to the failure of OAU policy. Surprisingly, on the Angola issue, Amin took the more conservative side, cleaving closely to the US and especially the Chinese line, and totally hostile to the Russians and Cubans (see above). Stated bluntly, Amin was Mobutu's ally: both leaders on several occasions publicly supported each other's stand on the handling of the crisis.[89] It was also the view of the MPLA that Amin was Mobutu's man, and this made them suspicious in all their dealings with the OAU.[90]

There are many interpretations of the reasons behind the Mobutu/Amin alliance, all of which go back to the Kampala Summit where the Zaire leader helped to turn the scales in favour of Amin against those who were boycotting the meeting.[91] Whether this is a sufficient explanation for Amin's devotion to Mobutu or whether there are other reasons is not yet known. The fact remains that Mobutu could not have found a more pugnacious ally than the OAU Chairman.

Amin's first act as Chairman was to appoint ten members to a fact-finding Committee of Enquiry and Conciliation to visit Angola.[92] They were drawn from Algeria, Burundi, Ghana, Kenya, Lesotho, Morocco, Niger, Somalia, Upper Volta and Uganda. (Morocco in fact played no part.) After a ten-day visit the Committee produced a report and recommendations[93] which were considered by the OAU Bureau (the committee which operates between summit meetings) in Kampala on 1 November. The Bureau again endorsed the need for a Government of National Unity composed of representatives of all three liberation movements, the integration of their armed forces into a single national army and suspension of armed hostilities—in fact, the same package as was produced by the Nakuru talks.[94] None of the Angolan representatives attending the Bureau's meeting was willing to commit his movement to proposals for an Interim Government. Significantly, the OAU committee reported that Unita had most popular support followed by FNLA with MPLA having the least.

On 5 November, Amin convened the OAU Defence Commission to consider the serious situation in Angola a week before its independence. Amin was pushing the idea of sending an OAU Peace-keeping Force, but the MPLA was strongly opposed. The Defence Commission agreed that the situation called for a political rather than a military solution. They considered the role of mercenaries in Angola; condemned the 'presence of SA and Portuguese troops in Angola as an act of aggression'; and expressed 'serious concern over the supply of arms to the warring Angolan nationalist movements', with its threat of internationalizing the problem. Finding itself without any active role to play in the unfolding violent issues, the Defence Commission appointed an *ad hoc* Advisory Military Committee (Egypt, Guinea, Kenya, Libya, Nigeria and Uganda) to assist Chairman Amin's consultations with the Angolan leaders about sending a Peace-keeping Force to maintain security, or, alternatively, an African political mission to 'help the Government of National Unity' to establish a national army and an administrative structure.[95] In his report to the OAU's emergency Summit in February 1976 on the work of the Bureau and the Defence Commission, the OAU Administrative Secretary-General, William Eteki Mboumoua warned:[96] 'If the present situation remains unchecked there are possibilities of an escalation of foreign intervention and dismemberment of the country. Already the situation in Angola is complicated by the presence of SA, Rhodesian and Portuguese mercenaries . . . SA and some other Powers would continue to endeavour to aggravate the situation by internationalizing the crisis in Angola. Such action is a flagrant violation of the Charters of the OAU and UN and could threaten the national independence and territorial integrity of Angola, the future of Namibia and Zimbabwe. Therefore it is vitally important that the OAU should identify all those who have intervened in Angola, whether directly or indirectly and consider ways and means, including official representation to those countries or Powers where possible, of putting an end to foreign intervention in the internal affairs of Angola. This will be a positive step in the OAU's efforts to create the necessary favourable atmosphere for a possible political solution of the problem of Angola.'

The MPLA's relations with Amin had deteriorated to the point of finding a flimsy pretext for not attending a meeting called by Amin in Kampala on 5 November, which both FNLA and Unita attended. Holden told Amin that the FNLA had 'no hate for the Soviet Union, but what right,' he asked '. . . has a European country to interfere and meddle in African countries, especially in black Africa?' At this time Amin addressed an extraordinary message to President Ngouabi of the Congo saying he might wish to send 'Ugandan troops to resist SA', and that he would wish to pass through the Congo. The Congo was then the main military staging point for Russian and Cuban aid going to the MPLA. It was also on alert against the possibility of Zaire sending its army across the Congo into Cabinda. Since Amin was, by then, also regarded by the Congo as Mobutu's instrument of policy, Ngouabi's hostile reaction was predictable: he called for Amin's resignation as OAU Chairman, and accused him of wishing to send in his Ugandan troops because he was 'allying himself with SA and Nato, contrary to our OAU resolutions'.[97]

With only three days to go before Angola's independence, Nigeria issued a statement proposing that it should be delayed for another three weeks to allow for more time to find a solution. At the same time, the Nigerian Foreign Minister denounced Russia for its intervention in Angola.[98] There was, however, no support for the proposal to delay independence and, as described above, Angola celebrated its independence with the new State at war with itself. The OAU's unity began to crack when Algeria, Congo, Guinea, Somalia and the four former Portuguese colonies (Mozambique, Sao Tome and Principe, Cape Verde and Guinea-Bissau) all chose to recognize the MPLA Government.

Alarmed by all this, the Central African Foreign Ministers (Cameroon, Chad, Rwanda, Central African Republic, Sao Tome and Principe, Gabon and Zaire) at their meeting in Libreville from 16-19 November, declared that the 'extremely grave situation in Angola directly menaces peace and security' in the area and throughout Africa. They condemned 'all foreign intervention in Angola, no matter where it comes from . . .' A week later eight Heads of State (Mauritania, Gabon, Senegal, Togo, Uganda, Zaire, Burundi and the Central African Republic), who were meeting in Kinshasa for Zaire's independence day anniversary celebrations, called for an emergency OAU summit meeting; but it took until February 1976 to get the Summit together. By then, 21 of the OAU's 46 member-States had recognized the MPLA and Africa was virtually split down the middle by the Angolan crisis.[99]

Amin's chairmanship of the conference left no doubt about his personal opposition to recognition of a purely MPLA Government. In his passionate speech opening the discussion, Mozambique's President Samora Machel insisted that FNLA and Unita had forfeited their right to be considered any longer as genuine nationalist movements because of their 'open collusion with SA', and demanded that 'President Agostinho Neto be seated forthwith as the legal Head of State of Angola', Amin, speaking from the chair, promptly replied to the effect that he would refuse to order FNLA and Unita out until instructed to do so by the Heads of State.

President Senghor of Senegal and President Seretse Khama of Botswana took the lead in opposing Mozambique's stand. Sir Seretse described the situation facing the OAU in Angola as one 'not of national independence and the liberation of a people from colonial domination, but that of a state of war—aggression against the independent State of Angola by extra-continental regular and mercenary forces and by racist SA, and self-annihilation by the people of Angola themselves'. He went on to say: 'The spectre of Vietnam, Cambodia and Korea has hardly vanished from the scene for us to think it will not re-appear in Africa. We must therefore unequivocally condemn its foreshadowing in this area if Angola must not become the testing ground of modern weapons. The OAU has not renounced its stand contained in its earlier resolutions that the encroaching of one country upon the territorial integrity of another constitutes aggression, nor that foreign intervention and the use of mercenaries constitute a serious threat to peace in the African continent. We must not abdicate our responsibility of seeking an African solution to an African problem.'

The pro-MPLA group got powerful support from Nigeria's then Head of State, General Murtala Mohammed, who completely reversed his country's earlier critical attitude to Russia for intervening in Angola. The problem, he said, was no longer one calling for 'a simple solution in the African tradition. Rather it is a much deeper danger of extra-African Powers in collusion with the inhuman and obnoxious apartheid regime in Pretoria trying to frustrate the will of a people who, having sustained a heroic struggle against a most brutal colonialist repression, are on the threshold of a glorious dawn of national self-determination. If the neo-colonialists succeed in Angola, then our hopes for southern Africa, will have been dashed'. After accusing the Western Powers of having refused to take any action to dissuade the Pretoria regime, he criticized the US President for having 'taken it upon himself to instruct African Heads of State and Government, by a circular letter, to insist on the withdrawal of Soviet and Cuban advisers from Angola as a precondition for the withdrawal of SA and other military adventurers. This constitutes a most intolerable presumption and a flagrant insult on the intelligence of African rulers'. He continued: 'We are all aware of the heroic role which the Soviet Union and other Socialist countries have played in the struggle of the African peoples for liberation. The Soviet Union and other Socialist countries have been our traditional suppliers of arms to resist oppression, and to fight for national liberation and human dignity. On the other hand the US, which now sheds crocodile tears on Angola, has not only completely ignored the freedom fighters whom successive US administrations branded as terrorists, it even openly supported morally and materially the fascist Portuguese Government. And we have no cause to doubt that the same successive American Administrations continue to support the apartheid regime of SA whom they see as the defender of Western interest on the African continent. How can we now be led to believe that a Government with a record such·as the US has in Africa can suddenly become the defender of our interests?'

This last passage in the Nigerian leader's statement caused President Kaunda to say: 'Assistance to liberation movements must not be an excuse for establishing hegemony in Africa. In this respect, we should learn from the People's Republic of China. Among the socialist countries China is easily the leading source of material assistance in the liberation struggle. China's contribution is immense. The OAU asked the People's Republic of China for assistance, it gave it willingly,, but China has not sought to impose its will on the people of Africa. It has not sought to twist the arm of Africa by any means. In this context we in Zambia deeply regret the untimely death of Premier Chou En-Lai. We pay tribute to him for leaving behind a clean record. China helped the struggle in Angola, but it has no imperialist ambitions. It has therefore refused to be involved in the tragedy of the Angolan civil war.' After condemning SA intervention and demanding the immediate withdrawal of its forces from Angola, the Zambian leader then 'went on to speak of the 'dangerous intervention of Super-Powers and their allies.' 'In the history of independent Africa, this is the first time that thousands of non-African regular troops and heavy sophisticated military equipment have been brought in to instal one political party into power and in service of their hegemonic interests. This is a most dangerous phenomenon which constitutes a grave threat to the entire continent and the unity of Africa. The involvement and rivalry of Super-Powers in Angola must not be condoned by the OAU. While these Super-Powers are trumpeting the end of the cold war era, in their bilateral relations, they are at the same time sowing seeds of discord in Africa. Angola is now a theatre for their hegemonic rivalry.

'It is dangerous for Africa to side with one Super-Power for that is an automatic invitation to the other to get involved. The world is cruel. Time has come for us to reaffirm the basic principles of Pan-Africanism.

1. No intervention by foreign Powers in African affairs.
2. No interference in the internal affairs of other independent States.

All foreign intervention must cease and all foreign troops and equipment must be withdrawn from Angola. Africa must never be the instrument for furthering the objectives of any Super-Powers.'

The Summit ended as it had begun—in a state of complete deadlock, with half the members calling for immediate recognition of the MPLA as the legal Government, and the other half still insisting on the need for a Government of National Unity. While there was virtual unanimity on the need to condemn SA's role and to demand withdrawal of its troops, the members were evenly divided between those wishing to condemn all forms of external intervention and those wishing to endorse the positive role of Russia and Cuba, whose intervention, it was argued, was justified by the need to defend Angola from the 'racist SA and other imperialists'.

It took a little more than a month for the issues that could not be settled round the OAU conference table to be decided on the battlefield. On 11 February 1976 the

OAU Council of Ministers accepting MPLA's military supremacy, decided by a simple majority to recognize the MPLA as the legal Government. Only Zaire protested openly, calling the decision of the Council of Ministers 'illegal'. Zambia announced that it was still not prepared to extend formal recognition to the new Government in Luanda. 'In our view', the Zambian Government said, 'the MPLA victory is not really theirs. It is a Soviet-Cuban victory.'

THE ROLE OF THE AFRICAN STATES

Zaire's heavy involvement in Angola can be explained in terms of the country's own traumatic experience of the chaotic aftermath of its independence in 1960 when it became the victim of both foreign intervention and internal rebellion. Those experiences shaped Mobutu's ideas about the nature of Zaire's national interests. He had finally come to power after defeating the secessionist leader, Moise Tshombe; but his rival's strong gendarmerie force eluded him by going into exile in Portuguese Angola, where they remained as a constant threat to Zaire's eastern flank. Mobutu had developed an almost paranoidal suspicion about the role of communist countries—Russia as well as China—after they had given their support to rebellion in Zaire. He was also constantly reminded of the vulnerability of his mineral exports from Shaba (Katanga) to any disruption of the Benguela railway. These, then, were the main determinants of Mobutu's Angolan strategy. But there were also two other factors: a strong ambition to play the dominant role in the Central and West Africa regions; and a wish to possess or, at least, to control the oil-rich Cabinda enclave lodged between Zaire and the Congo. Mobutu's Angola strategy had two main objectives: to ensure that an independent Angola should march as closely as possible in step with Zaire and, in any event, that it should not become a threat to the kind of system which he wished to see established in the region; and to encourage Cabindan separatism—just as once his arch-rival Tshombe had encouraged Katangese separatism.

For Mobutu the 'enemy' remains Russia. He had come to terms with China in 1973, and he had learnt painfully but successfully how to manipulate the Western countries to achieve his own strongly nationalistic aims. He fears Communism and has fanatical obsessions about the threats to his regime from a Moscow-orientated (or, as he thinks of it, a Moscow-dominated) neighbour. For him such a threat was always incipient in the MPLA Marxist leadership. It was to counteract this threat that he helped to guide and strengthen FNLA. So, long before the collapse of Portuguese colonialism (which he was able to challenge seriously only after he had achieved a measure of stability in Zaire and had established his own power base), Mobutu had put himself in the position where he would inevitably be drawn into the internal affairs of an independent Angola. His only hope of not getting caught up in a struggle for power was to come to terms with MPLA—but their suspicions of his close relationship with Holden Roberto, rather than his own unwillingness to negotiate with them, ensured the defeat of every attempt made in this direction.

Despite his apparently strong power base, Mobutu's hold on power has never been assured; what he needs above all to maintain his position is to expand his potentially strong economy, which suffers from the vicissitudes of world mineral prices and from a serious failure to promote the rural economy. For all these reasons, a close relationship with a prospering Angolan neighbour and a share of Cabinda's oil wealth could mean the difference between success or failure for Mobutu's rule. His handicap was the weakness of his main Angolan instrument—the FNLA. When it came to the final test, it proved a broken reed. Mobutu could never contemplate using his own army to give open, effective support to FNLA forces because of the outcry this would cause in Africa and, more important, his uncertainty about the effects such an operation would have on his own officers. So he needed external allies to offset those of MPLA. For a time he got some help from China, but in the last resort, he needed the support of the Western countries, especially of the US.

When the Americans, too, failed to match the support given by the Russians and Cubans to the MPLA, Mobutu was left without the effective means to execute his plans. The failure of his policies produced exactly the kind of results he most feared: a hostile Government across his border which was, at least, militarily dependent on the foreign Power most feared by Mobutu. He was also left with a million Angolan refugees inside his own frontier—a potential source of future trouble—and with a substantial part of the Katangese gendarmerie still at large in Angola to scheme their vengeance.

Mobutu's own stand on Cabinda was set out in a speech on 20 May 1975 in which he said that 'Cabinda is not Angola; it is separated by Zaire'. He did not say that Cabinda must be independent, but that its people should be allowed to decide freely through a referendum what future they sought for themselves. His Foreign Minister later drew the analogy between Cabinda and Bangladesh.[100]

Mobutu had succeeded at one stage in persuading his neighbour, President Ngouabi of the Congo, to join with him in making a declaration about Cabinda to the OAU Council of Ministers meeting in Addis Ababa in 1975. But in the end Ngouabi came down on the side of Cabinda remaining an integral part of Angola. The Congo People's Republic, which lives in an uneasy relationship with its more powerful neighbour, was for many years the headquarters of the MPLA; and it, too, has a strong interest in Cabinda. During the Angolan civil war Brazzaville became the strategic centre for the Cuban-Russian military operations in support of MPLA. This role was bound to make relations even more difficult, at least for a time, between the two capitals, separated only by the width of the Congo River.

Zaire's relationship with its other neighbour, Zambia, has never been an easy one, despite a period—1972-4—when Mobutu appeared to have joined the 'Mulungushi club' with Presidents Kaunda and Nyerere. Although Mobutu and Kaunda were to some extent on the same side during the Angolan crisis, Kaunda never opposed the MPLA nor was he as closely committed to Unita as Mobutu was to FNLA. Like Zaire, Zambia has a strong interest in Angola's stability and especially in the secure passage of its copper exports to the sea along the Benguela railway.

Kaunda, however, saw the issues in Angola essentially as questions of principles which were set out in an official document:

ZAMBIA'S BASIC PRINCIPLES ON ANGOLA
1. PRINCIPLES OF PAN-AFRICANISM, NAMELY:
    (a) non-intervention by foreign Powers in any shape or form in African affairs;
    (b) non-interference in the internal affairs of independent African States in accordance with the Charter of the OAU.

2. PRINCIPLES OF GOOD NEIGHBOURLINESS:
We believe that Zambia can live and will live and co-operate with any Government which will be established in Angola. It can be MPLA. We assisted them during their struggle. Our people died for them, property destroyed for the cause of MPLA. But we can equally co-operate with Unita or FNLA or a combination of two or three parties in a Government of National Unity because we are not against any one of them. We know that Zaire and Zambia are neighbours and MPLA

33

cannot afford to deliberately create an enemy in Zambia which assisted it and which is not opposed to its aspirations in Angola. The importance of Lobito to Zambia is not questioned, but if that was the only issue, then of course we would have to place equal importance to Zaire as a country of transit. At the moment the port of Beira in Mozambique is open to Zambia. But Rhodesia, the country of transit, has its borders with Zambia closed. So we cannot use Beira via Rhodesia. What we desire in Angola is a good, peaceful, stable, united, strong and prosperous Angola. We will work with any Government in Angola to achieve these aims.

3. PRINCIPLES OF DEMOCRACY AND NON-ALIGNMENT:
We believe in democracy and non-alignment. Our policy on Angola must reflect our own at home. We, therefore, believe that we cannot usurp the right of the Angolan people to choose their Government. This is their prerogative. We believe, that even if the MPLA or Unita or FNLA were to overrun the whole of Angola and defeat the other parties in a conventional war, this is no proof of the popularity of the victor nor the unpopularity of the vanquished. Military victory by one party will not be a proof of the non-existence of the other political parties. It is merely proof of the military weakness of the vanquished or the lack of military resources or capacity.

4. THE PRINCIPLE OF LIBERATION VIS-A-VIS MAKING GOVERNMENTS:
We believe that the task of Zambia, like other independent African States, is the total liberation of Africa. We will assist in the liberation of all territories under minority rule. But we will not go beyond the threshold of any newly liberated territory to get involved in making Governments for a sovereign people. We have no mandate to impose on the masses of a newly-independent country a Government which is not of their choice in the name of liberation which has already taken place. We cannot extend our mandate to decide what type of Government the people of Angola must have. That is their prerogative. In our view MPLA victory is not really theirs. It is a Soviet/Cuban victory.

By pushing his principles to the point of refusing to recognize MPLA, Kaunda put his copper exports through Lobito into jeopardy. He also incurred the angry hostility of the Russians: not only had he shown an open preference for the Chinese attitude in his OAU speech (see above), but he warned against the 'tiger and his cubs' (Russia and China) stalking the continent. Kaunda strongly criticized foreign intervention in Angola, yet he refused to condemn the US for sending weapons to FNLA and Unita. In his view, the latter had every right to ask for US arms so long as the MPLA was receiving them from the Russians.[101]

The Angolan affair was especially painful to Kaunda because, for the first time, he found himself taking a different position from that of his close friend and ally, Julius Nyerere; though fortunately they remain friends. They had worked since 1972 to try and bring the three Angolan movements together, and they had agreed about the leadership qualities of Savimbi.

But, in the end—even before SA's military intervention—Nyerere came out on the side of his other close ally, Mozambique's Samora Machel, in recognizing the MPLA's claims. His decision was strictly pragmatic: since the three rivals had finally proved themselves irreconcilable, the best hope lay in helping the strongest group to win as quickly as possible in order to avoid the greater risk of an embittering civil war and chaos. This was the judgement of a hard-headed realist temporarily setting aside the kind of principles which Kaunda insisted should not be abandoned—the right of the Angolans to choose their own government and an insistence on non-intervention by foreign Powers in African affairs. To this last objection, Nyerere's reply was that the Russians were only continuing the role they had played during the liberation struggle. But what of the substantial increase in their military supplies—far greater than the Russians were willing to provide to fight the old colonial Power? And what of the role of the Cuban commandos? Nyerere's answer to these questions is that this type of aid could be justified once SA had penetrated Angola. And that leaves open the argument of which came first—the large-scale Russian and Cuban intervention, or that of the SA?

The Francophone African countries were divided in their attitudes to Angola; but the larger countries (Senegal, Ivory Coast and Cameroon) were against the MPLA. The Arab States, too, were divided—with Algeria staunchly supporting MPLA, and with Libya opting for Neto only after Egypt had begun to show its preference for the 'anti-Soviet' front—a policy in line with Saudi Arabia's. Militant little Guinea was the only African country to announce that it had sent troops to fight for MPLA,[102] but this was probably only a token force. Mozambique officially denied reports that Frelimo fighters had been sent to Angola, and the Congo spoke only of 'material and political support'.

The only other African Government to play an important role in the Angolan conflict was Nigeria. At first, the Lagos regime was strongly on Unita's side, having promised military support to Savimbi in the middle of 1975. The Nigerian Foreign Minister, in a statement on 8 November 1975,[103] 'deplored the support given by the Soviet Union to one of the liberation movements to declare independence unilaterally'. He said that such 'flagrant interference in the internal affairs of Angola was inimical to the African initiative to resolve the crisis . . . the Federal Government therefore calls on the Soviet Union and others of the same inclination to desist forthwith from further interference in the Angolan situation'. Yet two months later, as already mentioned, the Nigerian Head of State completely reversed this position in his address to the OAU Emergency Summit. One explanation for this *volte face* is that the invasion by SA had put a different complexion on the situation; but SA had 'invaded' on 23 October—more than two weeks before the earlier statement made by Nigeria's Foreign Minister. A different explanation can be found in the clash of views over this issue within the Nigerian regime itself.[104]

SOUTH AFRICA'S ROLE

For SA, the Angolan affair was possibly the most traumatic in its history since the Anglo-Boer war at the turn of the century. It was the first time the SA army had been committed to fight in an African war. The operations in Rhodesia were of a completely different order—there the SA were fighting alongside white Rhodesians in limited operations against poorly-armed guerrillas; in Angola they were fighting alongside Africans against forces equipped with modern weapons and well-trained Cuban soldiers. Because the SA's role was principally that of supporting inadequately-trained and armed African troops, and because they did not commit their substantial mechanized and air forces into battle, they were fighting well below their true strength. The outcome was a humiliating defeat for the side they had chosen to support. For the first time in their modern history, white SA soldiers ended up as prisoners of war in African hands—a complete reversal of what SA had come to expect. The ill-starred Angolan enterprise also set back, perhaps permanently, the attempt to achieve a detente with black Africa,[105] and it jeopardized the chances of early independence for Namibia on a basis acceptable to the world community. During the Angolan fighting, the territory was turned into a major military base for the SA army. But from SA's point of view the worst result of all was that the Vorster regime had failed to achieve the purpose to which it had committed its army: to provide the necessary leverage to force the withdrawal of the Russians and Cubans from the area. The failure of the whole enterprise left the SA regime without a single crumb of comfort—and, by contrast, the morale of black SA opponents of apartheid was boosted.[106]

The SA army, as is now known, were no strangers to the Angolan terrain; the Portuguese had allowed them to send in their forces up to a depth of 200 miles to root out Swapo guerrillas and to study Angola's guerrilla operations. Their first reported entry into Angola during the recent crisis was made at the end of August 1975[107] when they moved to defend the installations at Ruacana on the Cunene River, following a number of clashes between Unita and FNLA troops in a local struggle for military advantage. During this operation, the SA forces had engaged in minor skirmishes with both Unita and FNLA.

However, it is clear that SA had moved its forces across the border earlier than August from an admission by the Minister of Defence, P. W. Botha, made in Parliament[108] that SA's total casualties in Angola was 29 killed in action and 14 killed in accidents 'from 14 July 1975 to 23 January 1976'. According to Savimbi,[109] 'SA for some reasons of its own, invaded southern Angola in July 1975. Both Unita and MPLA troops attempted to repel this invasion, and both were militarily defeated in the Cunene.' He claims that the whole town of Ongiva (Pereira d'Eca) had been destroyed in the engagement. The first officially admitted intervention was in August 1975. Pretoria claims[110] it had informed the Portuguese Government on 12 August that, in accordance with the terms of a SA-Portuguese agreement guaranteeing water supplies, it had moved up a 30-man patrol to the Calueque pumping station. Later,[111] Botha said the troops were sent to protect SA workers at the Ruacana Falls hydro-electric scheme 'who feared they would become involved in fighting between rival Angolan nationalist groups'; but, he added, this action was taken only after the Portuguese had failed to provide the protection asked for. Lisbon firmly denied that the action had been taken with its knowledge, and claimed that the formal Note of 12 August had been delivered only after Angola's territory had been violated. In September, between 800 and 1,000 SA troops and armed helicopters moved c. 25 miles into Angola and occupied Ongiva (previously reported destroyed) and Rocadas, because, the SA authorities claim, Swapo guerrillas had blasted the site of a SA army camp on the Namibian side of the frontier with 'Russian-made rockets' on 1 September.[112] The SA Defence Minister claimed at this time that 'our troops are at strategic points along our borders, but we do not interfere in the affairs of others'. However, this statement was soon qualified by an explanation that 'non-interference' did not mean they would not react to 'terrorist attacks'. This explanation was a prelude to a number of attacks, inflicting heavy casualties, on Swapo camps. Neto at that time criticized Portugal for its failure to protest against SA's entry—a remark called 'slanderous' by Portugal's President; and an MPLA spokesman expressed fears in September that SA was not just planning to defend the river installations.[113]

Clearly, one of SA's objectives was to seek out and destroy Swapo guerrilla camps inside Angola, taking advantage of the country's troubles. Swapo has not disclosed the full extent of its casualties, but they must have been high; they did, however, report that 'hundreds of Namibians, mostly villagers', had been killed 'on the pretext that they were harbouring Swapo terrorists'.[114] But why did the Republic embark on its massive intervention on 23 October 1975, as described earlier?[115]

The total number of SA forces which crossed the border from that time were variously estimated at 12,000 by Swapo,[116] 5,000-6,000 by French military sources in Kinshasa,[117] and 4,000-5,000 by the MPLA Minister of Information.[118] An even lower estimate was given by the MPLA Prime Minister in the first week of December—'1,000 and rising fast'.[119] SA were not told about their army's role until 18 December 1975. An official censorship was imposed on the Press which resulted in an angry controversy; so although the SA public was not told *what* was going on, they were treated to a public discussion about *why* they were not being told.

SA's reasons for its earlier, small-scale interventions across the border seem straightforward: partly to protect the dam and installations on the Cunene River (vital to Ovamboland) after fighting had begun between the Angolan rivals; and a desire to cripple Swapo, their principal enemy in Namibia. The official answer to the question why SA decided to risk a large-scale intervention, was given by the Minister of Defence: 'SA is playing a limited role in Angola because Russia is involved in a campaign of militaristic imperialism in that country . . . We were prepared to leave it to the people of Angola to solve their own problems, but the Russians interfered because they want to control the sea route around the Cape of Good Hope and because they want to exploit the wealth of Angola.' Taking a similar line, the Prime Minister said that the Soviet Union's intention was to have 'a string of Marxist States across Africa from Angola to Tanzania.[120] This would have serious consequences not only for SA but for States such as Zaire and Zambia, and the Western world'. He warned that if the Soviet Union through 'the left-wing MPLA established a permanent presence in Angola, it would stand astride the Cape sea route'. In a subsequent interview,[121] after having described the type of weapons introduced into Angola by the Russians, Vorster remarked: 'Only big Powers can offset this arsenal, above all the 122 mm rockets. It is certainly beyond our limits.' This is a strange admission for a country that has invested so heavily in its defences—precisely in anticipation of a possible 'communist offensive'.

The dominant theme of the pro-Government Press and politicans was that SA was fighting the 'battle for the West', and that the West was letting SA down and betraying their own interests. Vorster appealed publicly for greater Western involvement 'to save the war-torn country (Angola) from communism'. 'Apart from protecting the substantial interests of the Ovambo people in the Cunene River scheme,' he claimed, 'our only involvement is that of the free world.' SA newspapers compared Angola with the Cuban missile crisis of 1962, and Government leaders called on the West not to 'leave SA in the lurch in the struggle against the advancing forces of international communism'.[122]

If SA had really expected the West to come out openly alongside the Republic, its Government had miscalculated badly; there is no evidence of any Western nations responding openly to SA's invitation. Was there any secret collusion between the US and SA, as the Russians and others have suggested? The only sign of this possiblity was an oblique reference in an interview given by the SA Minister of Defence who spoke of the approval of 'a major Power' which, for obvious reasons, he chose not to identify. Kissinger, on a number of occasions, firmly denied any foreknowledge of SA's intention to intervene, and the US called for the withdrawal of SA troops along with all other foreign troops in Angola. No final judgement about possible SA-US collusion is yet possible. However, there is evidence to support SA's claims that they were encouraged to intervene by a number of African States to prevent a 'Russian/Cuban victory'. Three of the African countries named as having played such a role are Zaire, Ivory Coast and Zambia. This allegation appears in a report[123] prepared for Senator John Tunney by one of his staff aides, Bill Coughlin, who quoted Dr Savimbi as his source. Savimbi is reported as saying that SA had become involved at his own direct request. He claims to have flown twice to the south to ask for assistance—to Pretoria to meet Vorster and SA defence chiefs, and later to Windhoek. According to Coughlin's report, Savimbi said SA had acted with 'painful correctness' and that, at no stage, had it intervened without the approval of African Governments, 'such as Zaire, Zambia and the Ivory Coast'. He explained that he had taken his own decision to seek SA assistance at the end of September when he realized Unita needed help against the Cubans. According to the report, he had personally asked Mobutu, Kaunda and Houphouet-Boigny to ask for secret assistance from SA. Coughlin's report suggests that SA official sources told Savimbi in December 1975 that SA was withdrawing its troops because it had not received the support it had expected from the US and that SA could not fight alone against the Russians and Cubans. No further reinforcements could be sent without asking the SA Parliament openly for them. Dr Savimbi said he then approached President Kaunda and told him he wanted to speak to SA himself. 'Kaunda agreed', and the meeting with Vorster took place in Pretoria about 20 December. SA promised Savimbi then that it would remain in Angola for a little longer, but that eventually it would have to withdraw.

Savimbi's 'confessions', if true, are remarkable and would throw a completely different light on both SA's role and Unita's. However, President Kaunda has categorically denied any truth in the allegation that he had ever approached SA to intervene; he added that, on the contrary, he was always strongly opposed to their doing so. The account of Savimbi's role in the Coughlin report is directly contradictory to an earlier official Unita account about SA intervention, in which the allegation about its involvement with SA is called 'a lie'. The truth about these and other similar statements is likely to emerge only gradually.

What seems likely on the basis of present information is that some Angolan leaders (certainly the FNLA and possibly Unita) and some African leaders (but not Kaunda) encouraged SA to intervene; and that Vorster expected to win either a 'blitzkrieg victory', which would enable him to withdraw his forces quickly after capturing Luanda—a bad miscalculation—or that SA would get US support if the Cuban-spearheaded attacks could be halted for long enough to allow the Ford Administration time to get Congress's support for intervention. But none of this happened. SA's intervention, in fact, achieved four completely opposite results. It led to greater shipments of arms from Russia and more combat troops from Cuba, which became so large that they could be stopped only by a really major commitment (as the earlier quotation from Vorster indicates). It provided a more credible justification (in African eyes) for the Soviet/Cuban role. It caused a number of African countries (led by Nigeria and Ghana) to abandon their earlier support for Unita, which marked the beginning of the collapse of OAU concensus. And it helped to discredit the anti-MPLA Angolan movements suspected of colluding with 'Africa's arch-enemy'. In brief, the SA decision led directly to the result that it was intended to prevent. It also showed white South Africans that their leaders' hopes of getting the West to identify themselves openly with the Republic in the 'struggle against communism' are not grounded in reality. The actual reality is that SA remains bitterly isolated.

By the end of January 1976 SA had begun to withdraw to positions along the border, and in March it withdrew completely after assurances (obtained through Moscow and London) that the Ruacana installations would be safe. The Angolan adventure, as Stanley Uys wrote in a sombre assessment of the bitter mood of the Republic on the morrow of the defeat of its strategy, weakened Vorster's position and had the effect of bringing together SA's various white right-wingers.

SUMMING UP

The Angolan crisis opened up a new chapter in international affairs. Even its origins were different from anything that went before: it was a country which came to independence without an internationally recognized government since the departing colonial Power had refused to hand over to any of the three rival claimants. The Portuguese decision had left a power vacuum which, in the normal course of events, would have been filled through a localized power struggle. The objective of the policy followed by the OAU was precisely to create conditions for finding an Angolan solution to an Angolan problem. Moreover, finding an African solution to an African problem is a cardinal principle of Pan-Africanism; but in this, the OAU was openly defied by one of the two Super-Powers (Russia), and subsequently found itself internally divided once external Powers were sucked into the vacuum behind the three rival movements.

The principal elements which make the Angolan affair uniquely different from anything that has gone before are:

1. It was the first occasion when Sino/Soviet rivalry became the main determinant shaping both their policies towards a crisis in the Third World.

2. It was the first time that a foreign country—(Cuba) which is not itself a major Power—successfully introduced a major military force into Africa and, significantly, was not condemned by the OAU for doing this.

3. It was the first time that a Super-Power, the US, was actually prevented from playing a major role in an international crisis—not because its Administration did not wish it to do so, but because it was inhibited by its own public opinion—in the shape of Congress.

4. It was the first time that the SA army was committed to helping Africans fight Africans; and it was their first experience of their limited military power.

5. Finally, the outcome of the struggle further changed the balance of power in southern Africa.

It is not yet possible to fix with certainty the exact date when Moscow took its decision to commit itself to a major role in Angola; or when it first began to make arrangements with Fidel Castro for the Cubans to be given the role as bearers of the communist flag on the battlefield; or when it got President Ngouabi of the Congo to agree that his capital, Brazzaville, should become the military base for the build-up of Russian arms for MPLA and the staging-post for the trans-shipment of supplies and Cuban soldiers to Angola. Neither of these two latter arrangements could have been made at short notice; this suggests that careful thought had gone into planning the operation some time before the Russians first showed their hand.

Two facts are clearly established. First, the Russians were already engaged in sending substantial military supplies to MPLA by March 1975—six months before the first US arms shipments had begun to reach FNLA through Zaire, and two months after Kissinger had asked Congress to approve a limited military programme for this purpose. Second, the scale of the Soviet/Cuban intervention increased sharply in early October, which was three weeks before the SA forces entered Angola in any size. However, by September, the MPLA had become convinced that such an attack was likely. Because the Russians and Cubans had by then already established their communication lines to, and through, Brazzaville, it was a simple matter for them to increase the size of their intervention at quite short notice.

The March 1975 date is important because it shows that by then MPLA, reacting to Zaire's support for Holden Roberto, already felt sufficiently confident to meet and defeat the FNLA forces for control of the capital. By June the MPLA was sufficiently strong to take on Unita as well, and to spread its forces, albeit lightly, across twelve of the fourteen provinces.

Moscow seemed, at first, willing to support the OAU Summit decision taken in Kampala in July 1975 that the solution for Angola was to be found in a Government of National Unity which would include MPLA, FNLA and Unita. But it soon backed away from this position, showing its determination to get the MPLA recognized as the sole legal authority by its blunt demarche on the OAU Chairman, General Idi Amin, demanding that he—a heavy arms client of Moscow—should betray his own organization and follow the Moscow line. This was a remarkably clumsy, and hence ineffective, way of conducting diplomacy and it is evidence of the Soviet Union's determination to see its Angolan enterprise succeed.

Why did the Russians commit themselves so strongly? The situation in Angola in the early months of 1975 was that the MPLA faced an open challenge from the Zaire-backed FNLA. At that time the Chinese, with their military instructors based in Zaire, were FNLA's most effective backers. The US arms aid, which began to flow from January, was still on a small scale. If the Russians had wished to neutralize US aid, they had Kissinger's offer that both Super-powers should agree to stay out of the Angolan conflict. But to have accepted that offer would have meant leaving the field clear for the Chinese to 'spread their influence' through FNLA and Zaire. It would also have affected the Russians' relations with the Portuguese Communist Party (which at that time, they were backing heavily in Lisbon), which was strongly sympathetic to MPLA.

The propaganda war over Angola conducted in the Third World between Moscow and Peking shows clearly that the Russians were far more concerned about 'defeating' the Chinese than about undermining the West in Angola. It remains a moot point whether the Russians would have committed themselves so strongly—and further risked upsetting the Americans by introducing the Cubans at a time when detente was under considerable pressure in the US—if Congress had not signalled its clear intention of refusing to allow the Ford Administration to embark on yet another foreign involvement.

The Russian and Cuban contention that their military intervention was the result of SA intervention is clearly a *post facto* rationalization, since they were seriously involved before March 1975, and they had already put their aid programme into its second phase by the beginning of October—fully three weeks before the SA army had crossed the frontier. SA certainly provided the pretext they needed to justify their intervention on the respectable ground (in African eyes) of stopping the 'racist arch-enemy and its imperialist allies' from occupying Angola.

The Chinese, on the other hand, had made their decision to opt for neutrality as between the three rival movements in July when they immediately supported the Kampala decisions and announced their intention of withdrawing their instructors from FNLA camps. They gave as their reason for this decision that since they were not able to deliver aid to MPLA, they would have been taking sides if they were left supporting only FNLA and Unita. Two months later the Chinese, in fact, withdrew all their instructors from Zaire. The Russians, however, continued to accuse them of clandestinely arming the FNLA, but their evidence is unconvincing. They exhibited Chinese arms captured from the FNLA, but these could have been, and probably were, supplied while they were helping Holden Roberto's forces; and they repeated statements by Holden praising the help he was getting from the Chinese—but it is easy to show that all these quotations date back to the time when this was in fact happening. It is probable that Peking, taking a much longer historical view than Moscow of their role in Africa, believed that they would be able to achieve more by proving themselves loyal to OAU decisions. It is likely, too, that they did not expect the US to allow the Russians to oust them from an area of traditional Western interest; this is a view expressed to me by Chinese officials. Certainly, they were dismayed by what they came to regard as a sign of unpardonable US weakness in the Angolan affair and they said so to Kissinger.

Zaire's policies contributed directly towards creating the Angolan crisis. Mobutu's conceived national interest (or his own ambition) had led him into a policy of active intervention in his neighbour's affairs. Yet when the chips were down neither the FNLA nor the Zaire-backed Front for the Liberation of the Cabinda Enclave (FLEC) proved to be effective instruments in Zaire's cause. Mobutu's reliance on US support proved no more satisfactory.

The US, paralyzed by the aftermath of Vietnam and Watergate, failed for the first time in its recent history to behave like a Super-Power: Even its strongest card—reminding the Russians of the damage its Angolan policy could do to detente—was lighly brushed aside: another reminder that diplomacy between Super-Powers rests on the belief by both sides that they will really be prepared to use military power in support of political objectives. In any case, the US was always in a weak position in Angola because it had backed the Portuguese to win against the liberation movements; another case of birds coming home to roost. And the last man to complain about this should be Dr Kissinger since he had personally endorsed the National Security Memorandum 39, which proposed policies based on a momentously wrong judgement that armed struggle by Africans could not succeed anywhere in southern Africa.

SA's reckless decision to intervene with a part of its army succeeded only in ensuring the Soviet/Cuban/MPLA victory, thereby achieving precisely the opposite result to what was intended. Once again it was taught the painful lesson that even if Western interests were at stake, no Western nation would choose openly to accept the Republic as an ally 'in the fight against communism'. But the defeat of its intervention also brought consequences at home: the morale of black SA rose and Vorster's own stocks fell.

What of the two Russian arguments to justify their intervention—that they were supporting the legal Government of Angola (MPLA), and that the conflict was not a civil war at all, but a war of intervention? The easy answer to the first claim is that Portugal specifically refused, on laying down its colonial burden, to transfer its authority to any one of the claimants; and the OAU, speaking for the continent, inisisted that the only legal authority it was prepared to recognize was a Government of National Unity. The legitimization of the MPLA Government came from its success on the battlefield made possible only by the help of its foreign allies.

The second argument is purest sophistry. The struggle contained elements of both, as civil wars so often do. But, in Angola, the weight of foreign intervention obscured the nature of the violent conflicts among the country's three ethnocentric regions—and the Russian/Cuban contribution did as much, or more, than anybody else's to make it a 'war of intervention.'

The MPLA has every reason to feel grateful to the Russians and Cubans, but its future success will depend on the wisdom and skill of its able leaders in converting its military supremacy into a political authority resting on the consent of the Angolan peoples themselves.

NOTES

1. Quoted by Bridget Bloom in the *Financial Times*, London, 5 January 1976.
2. Written at the end of February 1975.
3. For earlier reference to FNLA see *Africa Contemporary Record (ACR)* 1968-9; *ACR* 1969-70; *ACR* 1970-1; *ACR* 1971-2; *ACR* 1972-3; *ACR* 1973-4; *ACR* 1974-5.
4. For earlier references to Unita see *ACR* volumes listed above.
5. For earlier references to MPLA see *ACR* volumes listed above.
6. For an excellent short statement of Angolan nationalism see John A. Marcum's Presidential Address to the African Studies Association (US) 'The Anguish of Angola: On Becoming Independent in the Last Quarter of the Twentieth Century'.
7. For earlier references to the Neto-Chipenda dispute see *ACR* 1973-4 p. B519; *ACR* 1974-5 p. B538.
8. *Radio Moscow*, 10 February 1976.
9. *Radio Luanda*, 2 February 1976.
10. Document entitled *Unita's Official Position on the War in Angola: The Internationalization of the War and Unita's Open Strategy for its Cessation.* Unita Information Office. December 1975.
11. *Star*, Johannesburg, 5 March 1975.
12. See *ACR* 1974-5 p. B539, C217.
13. For further details see chapter on Angola in *ACR* 1975-6.
14. See Document referred to in Note 10.
15. Savimbi's fears were expressed in a conversation with Colin Legum.
16. *Radio Lisbon*, 19 October 1975.
17. Leslie Gelb in *New York Times*, 25 September 1975.
18. *Financial Times*, London, 19 November 1975.
19. *Radio Kampala*, 10 November 1975.
20. *Ibid.*
21. *Ibid.*
22. *Radio Lisbon*, quoting an article from *O Jornal*, 31 October 1975.
23. Also see essay on *Russia's Year in Africa* in *ACR* 1975-6.
24. See Documents Section under OAU in *ACR* 1975-6. Also see Press Release No. 125 of the PRC mission to the UN, 13 November 1975.
25. *Radio Kampala*, 21 November 1975.
26. *Radio Peace and Progress*, Moscow, 1 October 1975.
27. *Tass*, 3 November 1976.
28. *Pravda*, 3 January 1976.
29. Statement by Professors F. Kozhevnikov, N. Ushakov, I Blishcaenko in *Izvestia*, 10 January 1976.
30. Tomas Kocesnichenko, *Tass*, 3 February 1976.
31. Valentin Zorin, *Moscow Viewpoint*, 7 February 1976.
32. *Izvestia*, 6 January 1976.
33. *Vladimir Iordanskiy, Tass*, 29 December 1975.
34. *Radio Peace and Progress*, Moscow, 6 January 1976.
35. *Radio Moscow* in Czechoslovakia, 26 January 1976.
36. 'Observer' in *Pravda*, 11 February 1976.
37. *Ibid.*
38. *Izvestia*, 27 December 1975.
39. 'Observer' in *Pravda*, 11 February 1976.
40. Brigadier W. F. K. Thompson, *Daily Telegraph*, London, 11 April 1975.
41. *Vienna Radio*, 29 January 1976.
42. Brigadier W. F. K. Thompson, *Daily Telegraph*, London, 11 April 1975.
43. David Martin, *The Observer*, London, 24 August 1975.
44. Dial Torgekson, *The Guardian*, Manchester, 27 November 1975, and A. J. McIlvoy, *Daily Telegraph*, London, 26 January 1976.
45. *The Guardian*, Manchester, 20 November 1975.
46. Also see Hugh O'Shaugnessy's *Castro's Foreign Legion in Angola*, Observer Foreign News Service, London, 25 October 1975.
47. Statement to his party congress, *Guardian*, Manchester, 16 February 1976.
48. *Financial Times*, London, 4 February 1976.
49. *International Herald Tribune*, Paris, 6 February 1976.
50. *AZAP*, Kinshasa, 20 December 1975.
51. *The Guardian*, Manchester, 16 February 1976.
52. Also see essay on China's Year in Africa in *ACR* 1975-6.
53. *AZAP*, Kinshasa, 27 October 1975.

54. *Daily Telegraph,* London, 28 November 1975.
55. See *ACR* 1972-3, p. C 28.
56. See *ACR* 1974-5 pp. B536, B538, C53-5, C58.
57. *Flash Nouvelles* FNLA, Kinshasa, No. 15, December 1973 and *The Observer,* London, 24 August 1975.
58. Statement by PRC Ministry of Foreign Affairs, Peking, 15 November 1975.
59. *Radio Peace and Progress*—in Arabic, Moscow, 6 February 1976.
60. *Radio Moscow* in Arabic to Algeria, 30 December 1975.
61. *Tass,* 4 December 1975.
62. *Peking Review* No. 39, 26 September 1975.
63. Statement by PRC's Foreign Minister, Chiao Kuan-Lua, to Zaire delegation in Peking, *The Times,* London, 18 February 1976.
64. Statement by PRC Minister of Foreign Affairs, Peking, 15 November 1975.
65. *Tass,* 17 November 1975.
66. 'Observer' writing in *Pravda,* 11 February 1976.
67. *Radio Peace and Progress,* Moscow, 16 January 1976.
68. *Radio Moscow,* 18 November 1975.
69. *People's Daily,* Peking, quoted in *International Herald Tribune,* 3 February 1976.
70. *Peking Review* No. 39, 26 September 1975.
71. *Tass,* 27 January 1976.
72. Also see essay on *US Year in Africa* for a fuller discussion of US policy in Angola in *ACR* 1975-6.
73. cf. Anthony Lewis in the *International Herlad Tribune,* Paris, 23 December 1975. 'Why do these men want to exaggerate the impact of distant events on their country's reputation?'
74. *International Herald Tribune,* Paris, 27 January 1976.
75. cf. Colin Legum: *An Open Letter to US Liberals;* New Republic, Washington, 31 January 1976.
76. *The Times,* London, 24 December 1975.
77. Kissinger's views were set out in the National Security Memorandum 39, see *ACR* 1974-5—*US Year in Africa.* Further evidence of Kissinger's policy will be found in official reports reproduced in *ACR* 1975-6, Documents Section/Political Issues under US and Africa.
78. See *ACR* 1974-5 pp. A97, A99.
79. See *ACR* 1974-5 pp. A87, B610.
80. See essay on *US Year in Africa* in *ACR* 1975-6.
81. Senator Frank Church, chairman of the Senate Select Committee on Intelligence Activities made this disclosure; *International Herald Tribune,* Paris, 15 January 1976.
82. Speech to Commonwealth Club of San Francisco, 3 February 1976.
83. *The Times,* London, 6 February 1976.
84. *The Guardian,* Manchester, 13 December 1975.
85. *Radio Club Portuguese,* 24 March 1975.
86. See essay on *Portugal's Year in Africa* in *ACR* 1975-6.
87. See *International Herald Tribune,* Paris, 3 February 1976 and 12 February 1976.
88. See essay on *OAU's Year in Africa,* also Documents Section, OAU Resolution on Angola in *ACR* 1975-6.
89. For example, see *Radio Kampala,* 7 November 1975, for Amin's endorsement of Zaire's policy.
90. For the attitudes of the Angolan leaders to the OAU chairman see Documents Section/Political Issues under Angola in *ACR* 1975-6.
91. See essay on *OAU's Year in Africa* in *ACR* 1975-6.
92. See Documents Section for OAU Resolutions on Angola *ACR* 1975-6.
93. The Report of the OAU Constitution Commission on Angola, Addis Ababa, January 1976.
94. See Documents Section/Political Issues under Angola in *ACR* 1975-6.
95. Memorandum of the OAU Secretary-General on the Situation in Angola, Addis Ababa, January 1976.
96. *Ibid.*
97. *Radio Brazzaville,* 18 January 1976.
98. *Radio Lagos,* 8 November 1975.
99. See essay on *OAU's Year in Africa* in *ACR* 1975-6.
100. *AZAP,* Kinshasa, 10 November 1975. Also see *AZAP,* 28 June 1975, for Mobutu's views on Cabinda given in an interview to the French magazine *Europe Outre Mer.*
101. See interview with C. L. Sulzberger in *International Herlad Tribune* Paris, 31 December 1975.
102. Statement by Guinea's Foreign Minister, *Radio Dar es Salaam,* 11 February 1976.
103. *Radio Lagos,* 8 November 1975.

104. See chapter on Nigeria in *ACR* 1975-6.
105. See essay on southern Africa: *How the Search for Peaceful Change Failed,* in *ACR* 1975-6.
106. See Denis Herbstan in *The Guardian,* Manchester, 23 January 1975.
107. *The Guardian,* Manchester, 4 September 1975.
108. *The Guardian,* Manchester, 26 January 1976.
109. Unita's official position, *op. cit.*
110. *The Guardian,* Manchester, 6 September 1975.
111. *The Times,* London, 9 September 1975.
112. *Daily Mail,* London, 5 September 1975.
113. *Guardian,* Manchester, 4 September 1975.
114. Statement circulated by Swapo at Extraordinary Session of OAU, Addis Ababa, 10-12 January 1976.
115. For a good description of the SA military role in October/November see 'The Reason Why'; *Financial Times,* London, 29 December 1975.
116. Swapo statement, see above.
117. *Daily Telegraph,* London, 13 February 1976.
118. *The Times,* London, 29 December 1975.
119. *The Times,* London, 19 December 1975.
120. *The Times,* London, 11 December 1975.
121. *International Herald Tribune,* Paris, 24 December 1975.
122. *The Times,* London, 24 November 1975.
123. *Ibid,* 17 February 1976.

PART THREE

HOW THE MPLA WON IN ANGOLA

TONY HODGES

How the MPLA Won in Angola

On 15 January 1975 the Portuguese Government signed an independence agreement at Alvor[1] with the three Angolan nationalist movements, the Popular Movement for Liberation (MPLA), the National Front for Liberation (FNLA) and the National Union for Total Independence (Unita). But the accord—a delicate attempt by Lisbon to promote a working political relationship among the three rivals and to fuse their armies prior to independence—set for 11 November 1975—was a gamble from the outset; it failed. Independence saw Angola engulfed in civil war and the proclamation of two republics—the MPLA's People's Republic of Angola (PRA), based in Luanda; and the Democratic Popular Republic of Angola (DPRA)—set up in Huambo by Unita and the FNLA. It took another three months of war for the MPLA finally to crush its rivals and establish the PRA's authority in all the major towns.

POLITICAL AFFAIRS

THE ALVOR AGREEMENT
The Alvor accord pledged the MPLA, the FNLA and Unita to work together with Portugal in a coalition Transitional Government during the ten-month interim period to independence. The Government, established on 31 January 1975, was headed by a Prime Ministerial Council of three members, one from each of the movements. Each also had three seats in the Council of Ministers, and Lisbon appointed a High Commissioner to arbitrate differences within the coalition. Government decisions would require a two-thirds majority. Machinery was established under the accord to integrate the liberation movements' armed forces into a single national army. A 10-member National Defence Commission, headed by the High Commissioner, was appointed, with representatives from MPLA, FNLA, Unita, the Portuguese army, navy and air force. The Commission's task was to oversee the integration of 8,000 soldiers from each of the liberation movements and 24,000 Portuguese troops into a mixed military force. When this was achieved, the Portuguese troops would be gradually withdrawn between 1 October 1975 and 29 February 1976. Finally, the accord committed the Transitional Government to draft a provisional constitution, draw up an electoral law and register voters and candidates for general elections to a Constituent Assembly. Elections were due to be held before the end of October 1975.

THE TRANSITIONAL GOVERNMENT (as of 31 January 1975)

High Commissioner	Brigadier-General Silva Cardoso (Portugal)
Prime Ministerial Council	Lopo do Nascimento (MPLA)
	Johhny Eduardo Pinnock (FNLA)
	Dr José N'Dele (Unita)
Ministers:	
Information	Manuel Rui Monteiro (MPLA)
Economic Planning and Finance	Dr Saidi Mingas (MPLA)
Justice	Dr Diógenes Boavida (MPLA)
The Interior	Eng N'Gola Kabango (FNLA)
Health and Social Affairs	Dr Samuel Abrigada (FNLA)
Agriculture	Eng Mateus Neto (FNLA)
Labour and Social Security	Eng António Dembo (Unita)
Education and Culture	Dr Eduardo Wanga (Unita)

National Resources	Eng Jeremias Kalandula (Unita)
Economic Affairs	Dr Vasco Vieira de Almeida (Portugal)
Public Works and Town Planning	Manuel Resende de Oliveira (Portugal)
Transport and Communications	Joaquim Antunes da Cunha (Portugal)

HOW THE ALVOR AGREEMENT BROKE DOWN

Although the nationalist leaders were committed to implementing the agreement, their long-standing rivalries did not end with the approach of independence; the struggle for power continued in a running battle of insults, slanders and even physical attacks against each other. As with the previous agreements between FNLA and MPLA in 1966 or the Supreme Liberation Council of 1972, none of the new agreements survived their signature.[2] The conflict tended increasingly during the year to assume a *de facto* ethno-regional character, as each of the rivals mobilized the inhabitants of its regions. The MPLA tapped its main base of popular support among the 1.5 m Mbundu concentrated around the Cuanza valley and the shanty-town dwellers of the Luanda *muceques* (sand slums). Unita rallied its strength in the south, in particular the 2 m Ovimbundu of the districts of Bie, Huamba and Benguela. The FNLA mobilized its traditional supporters among the half million Bakongo in the north-west and another half million or more Angolan Bakongo refugees in southern Zaire. But factionalism not ethnic hostility was the root cause of the spiralling violence between the movements. All three parties had Angolan nationalist perspectives, born of the experience of colonialism; all vehemently denounced tribalism and regionalism; all had multi-ethnic leaderships; and none relied exclusively for support on a single ethnic group. For example, FNLA's assistant secretary-general, Daniel Chipenda, is an Ovimbundu and succeeded in attracting some support in the south. Unita won support of non-Ovimbundu southern groups like the Cuanhamas, while two Cabindans are in its top leadership (Miguel Nzau Puna, the secretary-general, and José N'Dele, its representative on the Prime Ministerial Council). And MPLA's support went beyond the Mbundu to the southern port of Benguela; it had support among the Lunda, Chokwe and other Angolans in its old eastern guerrilla zones; and especially from the intellegentsia of all ethnic backgrounds and *mestiços*. All three movements, but particularly Unita and the MPLA, attracted white support. Nor were political principles or ideologies an important factor in deepening the conflict. The Angolan Ministers in the Transitional Government agreed on virtually all major policy issues: they favoured a united Angola and rejected separatism; all opposed the attempts of the Front for the Liberation of the Enclave of Cabinda (FLEC) to set up an independent Cabinda; all agreed on a broad statement of economic policy.[3] For example, on 10 May, the Minister of Economic Affairs, Dr Vasco Vieira de Almeida, announced that the Transitional Government had voted unanimously to adopt an economic programme proposing a 51% State control of the oil, gas, diamond, uranium, iron, wolfram, gold and copper industries but pledging that 'foreign capital will not be excluded from participating in the development of the country.'[4] All three movements opposed the wave of strikes which wreaked havoc on the Angolan economy, particularly the ports, in the latter half of 1974 and the early months of 1975. On 3 February, the Council of Ministers unanimously agreed to appeal to the 'worker and trade union organizations to suspend all their strikes until the necessary regulations and measures safeguarding the rights of the working class are passed and adopted by the Transitional Government.'[5] Later in the month all the Ministers unanimously voted in favour of a *Lei de mobilizacao* (mobilization law), allowing the Government to 'mobilize workers and place them under military control, discipline, and jurisdiction.'[6]

Notwithstanding this broad area of agreement the nationalist leaders, deeply mistrustful of each other, jockeyed for position and, placing their own narrow factional interests over those of the Angolan nationalist movement as a whole, rapidly became embroiled in a fratricidal struggle for supremacy. As the conflict escalated, each movement competed desperately for support from foreign Governments to provide the military hardware, and later the personnel, needed to defeat or block its rivals. The FNLA had, from the beginning of its struggle in 1961, relied for support on Zaire and it was difficult to distinguish its interests from those of President Mobutu. Since 1973 it had also had China's backing. The MPLA had always attracted some support from the Soviet Union and, for a period, also from China. Only Unita had no foreign backers before the collapse of Portuguese colonialism. China was the only major power that heeded OAU pleas and withdrew its instructors from the FNLA's camps in southern Zaire in late September 1975. Portugal, wracked by its own internal crises, was unable to act decisively to salvage the Alvor Agreement.[7] By deliberately externalizing their power struggle, the three rivals found themselves divided into pro-Western and pro-Russian camps, with FNLA and Unita in the first category and MPLA in the second.[8]

Ideologically, however, the MPLA was, like its rivals, essentially a nationalist movement; it repeatedly repudiated the Marxist label pinned to it by Western journalists and politicians and, demagogically, by its nationalist rivals. 'MPLA is not a Marxist-Leninist organization,' its President, Dr Agostinho Neto, said in an interview.[9] 'Also, our leadership is not Marxist-Leninist. Some of us have read Marx and Lenin, but we don't consider ourselves Marxist-Leninists. We are a large organization with various shades of opinion and different types of groups united solely under the flag of liberation. As a heterogeneous organization, it contains both Marxist and other points of view. But it is true that many people in the world consider the MPLA as a movement linked with Moscow. Again, I say this is untrue. This image exists only in the imagination of outsiders.'

THE FIRST WAVES OF FIGHTING

Indicative of the factional character of the whole ensuing chain of events was the first major physical clash after the investiture of the Transitional Government: an MPLA assault on 13 February 1975 against the Luanda offices of the movement's expelled 'Eastern Revolt' faction, a grouping led by ex-MPLA military commander Daniel Chipenda.[10] The MPLA attack, which succeeded in driving the Chipenda group out of Luanda and killed 15-20 of its members,[11] was justified on the ground that the 'Eastern Revolt' faction had not been recognized as a liberation movement by the Alvor conference and was therefore illegal. In fact, the assault was motivated by MPLA's determination to prevent a potential rival from establishing a presence in the capital. The attack drove Chipenda to seek the legal status bestowed by membership of a recognized liberation movement so, a few days later, he announced that his troops would join the FNLA.[12] On 15 April, he was formally admitted to the Front, voted onto its Revolutionary Council and Political Bureau, and elected assistant secretary-general.

Fighting also rapidly erupted between the MPLA and the FNLA. In the early months of 1975, the FNLA was acutely conscious of its political weakness in the country, above all in MPLA-dominated Luanda. The Front's support (until the fusion with Chipenda's forces) was concentrated almost exclusively among the million northern Bakongo, half of whom were living abroad in refugee settlements in Zaire. The FNLA tried to overcome this unfavourable relationship of forces, particularly in the strategic capital area, by setting up a well-financed political apparatus and sending well-armed contingents of its armed wing, the ELNA (Angolan National Liberation Army), into Luanda and other important centres.

With funds supplied by Zaire and the US the FNLA bought up the country's major means of communications, acquiring a TV station and the leading daily newspaper, *A Provincia de Angola*, reinstalling as its editor Rui Correia de Freitas who had previously been exiled after being accused of complicity with the 28 September 1974 right-wing coup attempt in Portugal.[13] At the same time, the FNLA launched a political offensive against the powerful pro-MPLA *Commissoes Populaires de Bairro* (Popular Neighbourhood Commissions) in the Luanda *muceques*.[14] The FNLA vigorously condemned a 'Week of Popular Power' organized by the commissions in the last week of January 1975. 'Having firmly decided to maintain law and order in Angola at all costs, because independence does not mean anarchy,' the FNLA warned on 2 February that 'all agitators for the so-called Week of Popular Power who forget that power should only be exercised by the liberation movements are outright enemies of Angola and must thereby be vigorously denounced by true Angolans and by our Press, which has the duty of serving our country.'[15] More important, the FNLA began to move large numbers of heavily-armed ELNA troops from its base camps in Zaire into Angola, including hostile Luanda. On a simple military level, the FNLA had a distinct advantage over its rivals at this time. While the MPLA had built up a relatively small guerrilla army of c. 6,000 soldiers, (Unita had an even smaller guerrilla force of, at most, 1,000), FNLA had trained a regular army of c. 15,000 troops in its Zairean camps.[16] In addition, it was well supplied with arms, having received 450 tons of Chinese weaponry in 1974, and it had the assistance of 125 Chinese military instructors.[17] There is evidence to suggest that the FNLA toyed with the idea of staging a direct military bid for power to compensate for its political weakness inside the country. The FNLA's Prime Ministerial Council Member Johhny Eduardo Pinnock, for example, was quoted in April as saying that several FNLA leaders 'almost came into conflict with the President (Holden Roberto) by trying to force him to wage war against the MPLA with all the machinery available. The President refused to let us do so, saying that when the time came the war must be between two armies, without the civilian population in the middle.'[18] Indicative of the FNLA's military build-up in Luanda was the arrival of a motorized column of 500 ELNA troops on 30 March.[19] Minor clashes between MPLA and FNLA occurred in February, but the first big conflict came on 23 March, when FNLA units attacked MPLA installations at Cazenga and Vila Alice in Luanda. Three days later, at Caxito, 30 miles north-east of Luanda, 51 young MPLA recruits were reportedly massacred after being seized by the FNLA.[20] Fighting raged in the Luanda *muceques* for days, despite a ceasefire agreement on 28 March and a further truce on 8 April. On 9 April, shooting broke out at Luanda airport shortly before Neto was due to arrive from Lisbon.[21] A second wave of battles followed at the end of April. In the early hours of 28 April, FNLA launched a co-ordinated series of assaults against MPLA headquarters in nearly all the *muceques* of Luanda and against the headquarters of the pro-MPLA trade union UNTA (National Union of Angolan Workers). The shootings, which led to the cancellation of a planned May Day march by UNTA, left 700 killed and 1,000 wounded by 3 May.[22] Meanwhile, fighting also erupted in the north—in Sao Salvador, Ambrizete and Tomboco—according to Neto.[23] In the south, fighting was reported between the FNLA and the MPLA at Nova Lisboa (Huambo) on 12 May and, further east, at Luso, Silva Porto and Teixeira de Sousa. Unita was involved in the factional fighting for the first time when its headquarters in Lobito came under MPLA fire on 20-21 May.[24] The Luanda fighting came to another temporary halt after the liberation movements signed a new ceasefire agreement on 12 May during an emergency visit to the country by the Portuguese Foreign Minister, Melo Antunes. The 12 May agreement came to an abrupt end 16 days later when a third more serious wave of clashes began. The

National Defence Commission charged on 1 June that MPLA had launched co-ordinated assaults against FNLA in Cuanza Norte and Malanje districts, east of Luanda. MPLA claimed it was retaliating after months of aggression by FNLA. FNLA responded by mounting attacks against MPLA in its northern strongholds, in particular at Carmona, the capital of the coffee-producing districts of Uige. Heavy fighting also broke out between the two movements in the oil-rich enclave of Cabinda on 3 June.[25] In two days of fighting, in which FNLA was driven out of the enclave's capital, eleven MPLA and FNLA members were killed, including the MPLA Central Committee member Gilberto Teixeira da Silva. On 5 June, the fighting spread to Luanda. The Sao Paulo hospital was shelled and mortar attacks were launched against both FNLA and MPLA headquarters in the *muceques*.[26] The fighting eventually subsided after a ceasefire between the movements on 7 June,[27] though further battles were reported at Santo Antonio do Zaire on 8 June[28] and at Henrique de Carvalho a few days later.[29].

The fighting in Luanda in early June affected Unita seriously for the first time. Of all the movements, Unita was the weakest militarily and had the least to gain from involvement in a military power struggle; so until August it concentrated on winning political support from the population by projecting itself as the 'party of peace'. However, much as it tried to steer clear of the fighting, it found itself caught up in the Luanda battles: its offices were attacked and several of its members killed by MPLA forces.[30] By then, the Alvor Accord was in disarray. The Transitional Government was hardly functioning. The provisional constitution, which should have been ready by 31 March, had still not been published. The electoral law, due to be published in April, had not been approved. There was not even agreement over how many refugees lived in Zaire and so how many would be allowed to vote in the elections. The UN, Unita and the MPLA estimated 650,000. FNLA claimed nearly 1.5 m. By the end of April only 300,000 had returned to Angola, according to the Health Minister, Samuel Abrigada, on 13 May. Only $8 m of the $150 m estimated necessary for resettlement had been allocated. Another complication arose as thousands of Africans fled the factional fighting to seek refuge in their home regions. Southern coffee plantation workers, for example, fled from the northern coffee estates to return home to Bie and Huambo.

The liberation movements had taken dozens of prisoners during the fighting and refused to release them despite paper agreements to do so. The mixed military units proposed by the Alvor Agreement had not been formed, and all the movements were recruiting as fast as they could. MPLA accused the Zaire Government of allowing weapons to pour across the border for the FNLA, while FNLA accused MPLA of receiving arms shipments by sea from the Soviet Union.[31]

THE NAKURU AGREEMENT AND ITS BREAKDOWN

Anxious to resurrect the Alvor accord and weld together a unified government and national army prior to independence, the Portuguese regime pursued its policy of 'active neutrality' between the battling rivals. At the same time, the OAU and virtually all African Governments pleaded with the three movements to observe immediate ceasefires, patch up their differences and adhere to the spirit of the Alvor Accord. In January 1975 all three liberation movement leaders met under President Kenyatta's chairmanship in Mombasa and signed a strict endorsement of the Alvor Agreements.[32] But by 14 May it had once again become necessary for the Portuguese Government to summon the three leaders for a virtual re-run of the Alvor Summit. Unita's president, Dr Jonas Savimbi, emerged as the strongest proponent of a peaceful settlement of the conflict, winning him increasing backing from African Governments. In the last week of May, he began a week of capital-hopping that ended with the announcement that the three movements' presidents would meet again in Kenya to thrash out a settlement and salvage the Alvor Accord. Neto, Savimbi and Roberto accordingly met at Nakuru in Kenya from 16–21 June. This time, the Portuguese Government was not invited—Roberto had categorically rejected participation in a Summit which included the Portuguese because, he charged, the Armed Forces Movement was biased in favour of MPLA.[33]

On 21 June, the three presidents signed an agreement 'with a view to restoring a climate of peace in Angola.'[34] But the ink was hardly dry on the agreement before shooting broke out again among the movements, with mortar fire and shooting in Luanda on 23 June. The High Commissioner, Brigadier-General Silva Cardoso, accused both MPLA and FNLA of violating the agreement.[35] Symptomatic of the low chances for success expected from the agreement at the time was the release in the first week of July of a letter to the presidents of the three movements from the Minister of Economic Affairs, Dr Vasco Vieira de Almeida, in which he warned that the country was on the brink of economic and political collapse and that 'the survival of Angola as an independent and unitary State is at stake.'[36] The first week of July saw a modest attempt to implement the agreement. The Transitional Government published the long-awaited provisional constitution on 6 July.[37] The first company of the new Angolan national army was inaugurated in Cabinda on 5 July,[38] and in various parts of the country leaders of the liberation movements participated in a Unity Week.[39] But on 9 July a fourth major wave of fighting erupted, pushing the nationalist movements to the verge of total civil war and, for the first time, beginning to divide the country up into military spheres of influence. The National Defence Commission, meeting without its MPLA members on 12 July held MPLA 'responsible for the widespread nature and escalation of the incidents taking place in Luanda.'[40] By 14 July, MPLA had driven FNLA out of Luanda except for three small pockets of resistance in the old fortress of Sao Pedro da Barra and in the Cuca and Cazenga suburbs. Elsewhere in the city, FNLA installations had been gutted or seized by MPLA. But the MPLA offensive was not limited to the capital. It involved an obviously well-prepared and co-ordinated drive to eject FNLA from all its traditional political strongholds in the Luanda-Malanje corridor, and even further east in Lunda. Battles raged in Dalatando, Malanje, Lucala, Henrique de Carvalho and other towns. By the end of the month, MPLA had succeeded in asserting its unchallenged control over the entire centre of the country, running eastwards from Luanda to the Zambian border. FNLA was driven back into the north-west of the country.[41]

MPLA was able to launch such a calculated offensive in defiance of the Nakuru Agreement because it had received sufficient military supplies since March 1975 to undercut the military advantage held by FNLA in the early months of the year. In March, several Soviet planes had delivered arms to MPLA in Congo-Brazaville, from where they were smuggled into Angola. In April, 100 tons of arms had been delivered to MPLA in southern Angola by chartered aircraft. In April, two Yugoslav vessels had delivered arms. And in May and June, four Soviet ships had landed arms. Other supplies arrived in two East German and one Algerian ship.[42]

With its troops driven out of the capital, FNLA decided to launch a counter-offensive from its strongholds in the northern districts of Zaire and Uige, where it now had c. 17,000 troops.[43] On 13 July, FNLA's headquarters announced that all its military units had been put in 'a permanent state of military alert'. Accusing the Portuguese of siding with the MPLA, the FNLA Political Bureau declared on 20 July that ELNA troops would march on Luanda and attack any Portuguese troops that tried to stop them. The next day, FNLA announced that Roberto had returned to Angola to lead his troops in the march on Luanda; this, remarkably, was the first

52

time he had set foot in the country for 14 years. Ceasefires arranged in a chaotic series of National Defence Commission meetings were immediately violated. On 24 July the FNLA seized Caxito, 30 miles north-east of the capital.[44] On the next day, Chipenda announced that 'our forces are marching on Luanda and we hope they will make their entry into the Angolan capital in the next few days.'[45] On 26 July, FNLA announced that Roberto had 'ordered a general mobilization of the entire Angolan people so that we can give battle to the murderous fury of social imperialism which is aiming to implant neo-colonialism in Angola'. Roberto, FNLA said, 'is advancing in the direction of Luanda, to smash completely the fanatical and lunatic bourgeois traitors of the notorious and death-rattling MPLA'. It ruled out compromise. As Chipenda put it on 25 July: 'We do not think that new negotiations are possible any longer; we are going to Luanda, not to negotiate, but to lead.'[46] And in Roberto's words on 29 July: 'We have signed a number of agreements, all of which have been violated by MPLA. Now we will no longer be tricked. Now we will go forward.'[47] MPLA's view was similar, as the Political Bureau member, Nito Alves, explained: 'We are 100% enemies and can never come to any agreement. Our fight must go on until FNLA is defeated as the American imperialists were in Vietnam.'[48]

By the first week of August, according to Unita, its forces too were coming under repeated attack from units of MPLA. It claimed that Savimbi's jet was shot at by MPLA soldiers in Silva Porto on 3 August—an action which led it to place its armed wing, the FALA (the Armed Forces for the Liberation of Angola) on full alert two days later. Heavy fighting ensued in Silva Porto until MPLA evacuated its troops from the town. Unita's secretary-general, Miguel Nzau Puna, also claimed that MPLA soldiers had massacred 150 Unita recruits on 9 August. After a major battle between FNLA and MPLA troops in the magisterial district of Luanda on 8 August—which prompted the Portuguese to accede to MPLA demands that FNLA's Ministers be evacuated from the capital—Unita also withdrew its Ministers and FALA soldiers from Luanda. Clashes between MPLA and Unita occurred in the Cunene valley area in the first week of August, and on 14 August major clashes started between them in Lobito and Benguela. On 16 August, Unita and MPLA were fighting in Luso. Finally, on 21 August, after concluding a party conference in Silvo Porto, Unita formally declared war against MPLA. In the next few days battles raged between the two movements. As the fighting spread, Unita forces were evicted from a string of southern cities—Luso, Benguela, Lobito, Mocamedes, Sa Da Bandeira and Pereira d'Eca. This reflected the fact that Unita was, militarily, by far the weakest of the three movements at this time, and that MPLA had by then received sufficient arms' supplies to feel strong enough to take on its southern rival as well as FNLA in the north. There was a final bid to bridge the gap between MPLA and Unita at the end of August. With Portuguese prompting, Lopo do Nascimento and Jose N'Dele met in Lisbon on 25 August for several days' talks; but nothing came of the negotiations.

THE SITUATION IN CABINDA

Separatists in the enclave of Cabinda, sandwiched between Zaire and Congo, hoped meanwhile to take advantage of the mounting chaos in Angola to push ahead with plans to set up an independent Cabindan State. On 1 August, Luis Ranque Franque, president of the Kinshasa-based Front for the Liberation of the Enclave of Cabinda (FLEC), declared the territory independent at a Kinshasa Press conference. Six days earlier, a rival separatist group led by N'Zita Henrique Tiago had announced in Paris that it had set up a 'Provisional Revolutionary Government' for the enclave.[49] But, with MPLA forces in firm control of Cabinda, neither announcement had any practical impact.

Zaire, while backing FNLA (which opposed Cabindan separatism), played a double game by aiding Franque's FLEC too. President Mobutu repeatedly declared that Cabinda was a separate entity from the rest of Angola and that a referendum should be held in the district to determine its future.[50] Gabon also recognized FLEC on 22 June after a meeting between Franque and President Bongo. The Congolese Government flirted with Cabindan separatism (in addition to aiding MPLA), giving some support to separatists opposed to the Franque faction.[51] The Congolese Foreign Minister, Henri Lopes, said on 29 April that 'Cabinda exists as a reality and is historically and geographically different from Angola'. He proposed a referendum. But later in the year President Ngouabi swung his support decisively behind MPLA's role in the enclave, stating in November that Congo would intervene to aid MPLA in Cabinda if 'mercenaries' entered the enclave.[52] But there was no serious challenge to MPLA hegemony in Cabinda either from FLEC or from FNLA.

THE ROLE OF PORTUGAL

Portugal, pursuing its policy of 'active neutrality', tried at first to increase its role in Angola. Its troop commitment in the country rose to 27,000 in mid-July.[53] Following a visit to Luanda, 12-14 May, Melo Antunes said that 'if the conflict escalates, the troops present at the moment in Angola will not be sufficient. In that case we will have to take political measures immediately.'[54] Returning to Luanda on 13 July, Antunes said that Portuguese troops 'will not fold their arms and look on, but will actively intervene very vigorously to put the aggressors in their place.' On 14 July, two transport planes flew reinforcements to Luanda and, on 17 July, Lisbon Radio announced that three companies of troops had left for Angola. On 26 July, Portuguese troops—dispatched by the Luanda Operational Command to MPLA headquarters in Vila Alice (Luanda) on a 'punitive' mission after an army vehicle had been shot at a day earlier by MPLA soldiers—opened fire, killing 14 and wounding 22. Two days later, in a major policy reversal for MPLA, Neto demanded the withdrawal of the Portuguese troops from the country.

The breakdown of the Nakuru Accord forced Portugal to attempt even greater intervention. On 1 August, an investigative mission led by General Carlos Fabiao and Admiral Rosa Coutinho was dispatched to Luanda and the High Commissioner, Silva Cardoso, was recalled to Lisbon against strong protests by FNLA and Unita who feared that his recall reflected growing pressures within the MFA to back MPLA. His replacement, General Ferreira do Macedo, after evacuating FNLA's Ministers from Luanda, announced on 14 August that he was taking over the functions of the Prime Ministerial Council. A new High Commissioner, Commodore Leonel Cardoso, was appointed on 28 August. The next day, Portugal formally annulled the Alvor agreement and announced the dissolution of the Transitional Government. The same week, Lisbon explored the possibility of setting up a Unita-MPLA coalition as a 'second-best' solution—by hosting talks between Jose N'Dele and Lopo do Nascimento (see above). Portugal's new initiatives failed. Unita and MPLA were in no mood to compromise. All three nationalist factions opposed the increased Portuguese role—for their own different reasons. MPLA Ministers in Luanda stayed at their posts despite the formal dissolution of the Government, while FNLA and Unita Ministers vowed to govern from Huambo (Nova Lisboa). Above all, Portugal's own domestic upheavals and the unpopularity of continued colonial involvement made it impossible for Portugal to intervene decisively. 'There are two main difficulties about any major Portuguese military operation in Angola,' one observer noted in May.[55] 'Troops stationed in the colony are badly demoralized and have little stomach for a fight. Those which have left have no intention of returning.' On 8 June, 76 soldiers mutinied in Lisbon against orders to board a plane for

Angola.[56] Protests by both soldiers and civilians intensified in Lisbon after 200 military police and 5,000 supporters marched through the city on 1 September demanding the withdrawal of troops. Antunes and other Portuguese leaders appealed on several occasions for UN or OAU intervention, but none was forthcoming.[57]

By mid-September, Lisbon felt it had little option but to get out of Angola. On 18 September, Leonel Cardoso announced that Portugal would start to withdraw its troops from the country and, on 28 October, the Portuguese Government announced that all its troops would be withdrawn before independence on 11 November.[58] In these last few weeks, the Lisbon regime was confused and divided on the course to pursue. One wing of the MFA hierarchy favoured outright support for MPLA and argued that Portugal should recognize the MPLA regime after 11 November. The most outspoken representative of this wing was Admiral Coutinho, who had served as High Commissioner in Angola before the establishment of the coalition regime.[59] But majority opinion in Lisbon was that the safest policy (especially in view of the military dangers facing MPLA at the time) would be to leave the doors open to co-operation with whatever nationalist force gained dominance. To this end, Lisbon decided against recognition of any of the factions.[60] Other actions, however, gave MPLA some valuable support: large quantities of Portuguese arms were left behind in MPLA areas by the departing Portuguese troops.

THE FIGHTING IN SEPTEMBER-NOVEMBER 1975

By the beginning of September, MPLA appeared to have the upper hand in the struggle. Controlling the capital, it had access to the Government apparatus and to sophisticated communications' equipment. It also controlled 11 of the country's 16 district capitals and occupied more territory than its rivals. Virtually the entire seaboard was in the movement's hands, including all the country's major ports (Cabinda, Luanda, Lobito and Mocamedes). It was by then receiving substantial Russian arms supplies.[61] Unita, by contrast, had been pushed back into the Ovimbundu heartland of Huambo and Bie—though clashes continued around Luso in September and October.[62] In the north, FNLA, despite the receipt of large shipments of US aid (conduited through Zaire) was unable to break through MPLA's defences and march back into Luanda. The nearest the ELNA troops got was Quifangondo, 15 miles to the north-east, where battles first raged on 30 August. From then on, the northern front was largely stationery for three months as FNLA and MPLA units successively captured and re-captured Caxito, Porto Quipiri and other villages on the approach roads to the capital.

The MPLA, however, was unable to inflict a decisive defeat on its rivals. Both FNLA and Unita were now receiving large arms shipments from the US and other sources, including African countries. By August, MPLA claimed, US arms were being flown direct from US bases in West Germany aboard Skymaster transport planes to the FNLA's airfield at Negage.[63] In July, the Forty Committee decided to send $60 m of covert aid to anti-MPLA factions[64]—and the Ford Administration lobbied Congress for approval of an $81 m aid package for Zaire.[65] Part of the US funds were used to recruit mercenaries for Unita and FNLA. And, in December, under State Department pressure, Gulf Oil stopped its substantial royalty and tax payments to MPLA. (See Economic Affairs below.) More important was the intervention of SA.[66] This took three forms: first, 'hot pursuit' missions across the Angolan border from Namibia to strike at bases of the South-West African People's Organization (Swapo); second, starting in early August, the military occupation of the strategic Ruacana Falls hydro-electric scheme and other installations on the

Cunene River;[67] and third, direct intervention into the Angolan civil war on the side of Unita and FNLA on the southern front from 23 October.[68] Like the US covert aid, the SA intervention was designed to engineer a military stalemate between the factions, thereby giving Pretoria powerful leverage with which to attempt to force concessions from them, particularly with regard to future Angolan policy towards detente in southern Africa and Namibia. The intervention of 1,500 to 2,000 SA regular troops, equipped with armoured cars, dramatically shifted the military balance on the southern front. By 26 October, the SA column had forced the MPLA out of Sa da Bandeira.[69] By the end of the month, the port of Mocamedes had fallen and, in the first week of November, the SA column drove MPLA out of Benguela and Lobito, 400 miles north of the Namibian border.[70] On 12 November, the SA captured Novo Redondo, 100 miles north of Lobito. These major setbacks for MPLA were to be reversed only some weeks after independence following the arrival of massive Soviet arms shipments and thousands of Cuban troops.

INDEPENDENCE, 11 NOVEMBER 1975

Independence Day saw the proclamation of two rival Governments. In Luanda, Neto was sworn in as President of the People's Republic of Angola (PRA).[71] In Ambriz, Roberto announced the formation of the Democratic Popular Republic of Angola (DPRA)[72] and, in Lisbon, Unita announced that a coalition Unita-FNLA Government would be set up in Huambo (Nova Lisboa).[73]

No foreign countries recognized the Huambo Government. Some recognized the MPLA regime: Brazil, Somalia, Mauritius, Mali, Guinea, Congo, Madagascar, Mozambique, Guinea-Bissau, the Cape Verde Islands, Sao Tome, Cuba, North Korea, North Vietnam, South Vietnam, Yugoslavia, the USSR and the other Comecon countries. The majority of African Governments, all the NATO countries and China were among those which decided not to recognize either regime—although the US, SA, Zambia and Zaire, while formally not recognizing the Unita-FNLA coalition, continued to assist its forces militarily. The OAU did not admit either Government to its ranks and called for. a ceasefire between the factions and the establishment of a government of national unity.[74] This was in line with policies set at the OAU's Summit in July, when a 'Conciliation Commission' was set up to try to bring the warring parties together. On the eve of independence, in Kampala, the Conciliation Commission met with representatives of the three liberation movements and proposed, on 5 November, the formation of a Coalition Government, the demilitarization of Luanda, the dispatch of an OAU peace-keeping force, the drafting of a constitution and the holding of elections, and the re-establishment of a Prime Ministerial Council.[75] MPLA rejected the plan and the OAU meeting broke up on 7 November with nothing achieved. Official OAU policy came under increasing challenge as Africans learned (after weeks of denials) that SA troops had entered the war on the side of Unita and FNLA. On 27 November the Nigerian Government announced its recognition of the MPLA regime, citing the SA role as its reason.[76] Tanzania followed on 5 December, also citing the SA intervention. By early January, several other African Governments had followed their lead.[77] An emergency Summit of the OAU, called to debate the Angolan crisis from 10-13 January, found African Governments split down the middle: 22 supported recognition of the MPLA regime, 22 maintained a stance in favour of a ceasefire and the formation of a Government of National' Unity. Ethiopia and Uganda abstained. The Summit broke up in deadlock.[78]

Faced with these setbacks, the Unita-FNLA coalition was rapidly revealed to be a feeble marriage of convenience between two mutually hostile parties, drawn together solely by their feud with MPLA. It took several weeks of hard bargaining for the two

56

coalition partners to thrash out the composition of their Government. Eventually, on 3 December, the Council of Ministers and a 24-member Revolutionary Council were officially installed. No attempt was made to fuse the ELNA and the FALA into a unified national army, and there were several clashes between their supporters in the south. Following clashes in Lobito and Benguela, the Unita-controlled *Radio Clube de Lobito* broadcast in late December that 'we guarantee the Angolan people that FNLA will be expelled from central and southern Angola within the next few weeks.'[79] At least 25 were reported killed in clashes in Huambo on 25 December.[80] There was also heavy fighting in Lobango (Sa da Bandeira) and Mocamedes on 29 December, in which FNLA's supporters were apparently driven out by Unita troops.[81] FNLA would not even allow Unita to operate in the north-western districts under FNLA control.

THE PRA GOVERNMENT (on 15 November 1975)[82]

Prime Minister	Lopo do Nascimento
Defence Minister	Commander Iko Carreira
Labour Minister	David Aires Machado
Foreign Minister	Dr Jose Eduardo dos Santos
Information Minister	Joao Felipe Martins
Interior Minister	Commander Nito Alves
Justice Minister	Dr Diogenes Boavida
Planning and Finance Minister	Carlos Rocha

Five more Ministers were appointed later.

THE DPRA GOVERNMENT (on 3 December 1975)[83]

Prime Ministers	Johnny Eduardo Pinnock (FNLA)
	Dr Jose N'Dele (Unita)
Interior	Matheus Katalaye (Unita)
Foreign Affairs	Hendrik Vaal Neto (FNLA)
Information	Dr Fernando Wilson Santos (Unita)
Education and Culture	Dr Eduardo Wanga (Unita)
Agriculture and Fisheries	Domingos Fernandes (FNLA)
Labour	Eliseu Chimbili (Unita)
Planning and Finance	Dr Graca Tavares (FNLA)
Economy and Commerce	Dr Jean-Paul Mouzinho (Unita)
Natural Resources	Isaac Jacob (FNLA)
Transport and Communications	Eng Antonio Dembo (Unita)
Industry and Energy	Eng N'Gola Kabango (FNLA)
Public Works	Joao Vahekeni (Unita)
Justice	Onofre Martins dos Santos (FNLA)
Secretaries of State:	
Foreign Affairs	John Marques Kakumba (Unita)
Information	Miguel Sebastiao (FNLA)
Planning and Finance	Luis Miguel Alfonso (Unita)

THE MPLA'S VICTORY

The entry of SA troops into the war on 23 October and the sudden reversal of military fortunes in the south prompted the Soviet Union to step up its arms supplies and Cuba to send thousands of troops to aid the MPLA. By mid-December, the USSR had sent 27 shiploads and 30–40 supply missions in An-22 cargo planes since the beginning of October.[84] By mid-January 1976, the MPLA was reported to be supported by 9,000 Cuban troops, 6,500 Katangese gendarmes and 400 Russian advisers. The movement had large numbers of 'Stalin Organs', 68 PT-76 light amphibious tanks, 10 T-54 tanks, 20 T-34 tanks, 12 MiG-21 jets and 3 FIAT 91 jets.[85] In January 1976, Dr Kissinger claimed that the USSR had sent $200 m of aid to MPLA during 1975. The American role roused widespread opposition in the US, and the SA intervention back-fired, prompting many African Governments to recognize the MPLA, and legitimizing in the eyes of many, particularly in Africa, the MPLA's use of Cuban troops and Soviet arms.[86]

These international developments allowed the MPLA to reverse the military situation dramatically from the end of November 1975. By 20 November, the SA advance from the south had been effectively halted on the River Queve, preventing Unita and the FNLA from reaching Porto Amboim, Gabela and Quibala.[87] On the eastern front, the war took a more fluid form. The MPLA captured Luso and Cangumbe from Unita at the end of November,[88] but Unita managed to retake them in mid-December.[89] Still, Unita suffered a serious blow when its forces failed to capture Teixeira de Sousa on the Zaire border, the last town on the Benguela Railway that it had earlier failed to take from MPLA. The shift in the military balance was strikingly demonstrated when MPLA began a major offensive against the FNLA's positions in the north in December. On 5 December, MPLA claimed it had driven FNLA out of Caxito and was advancing towards Ambriz. Advancing into the Bakongo heartland, MPLA announced on 5 January 1976 that its forces had captured the strategic FNLA airbase at Negage and the city of Uige (Carmona). On 12 January, MPLA went on to seize Ambriz. FNLA's defences had collapsed. In February, MPLA evicted FNLA from its last centres of résistance—Santo Antonio do Zaire (7 February); Maquela do Zombo (12 February) and Sao Salvador (16 February). An ill-prepared, last-ditch defence of these cities by British and other mercenaries ended in fiasco.

Following MPLA's gains in the north in January 1976, the movement turned its fire against Unita in the south. Deciding to cut its political losses and avoid the pending confrontation with MPLA, SA pulled its troops out of the front line, leaving Unita to fend for itself. The SA Defence Minister announced on 4 February that SA troops had been withdrawn to a 50 km deep *cordon sanitaire* on the Angolan side of the Namibian border.[90] The southern offensive began at the end of January. MPLA claimed to have captured Cela and Santa Comba by 21 January; Novo Redondo by 24 January; Alto Hama by 7 February; Huambo by 8 February; Lobito, Benguela and Catumbela by 10 February; Lobango by 11 February; Silva Porto by 12 February.

Recognition followed rapidly in the wake of MPLA's territorial gains. 25 African States had recognized the PRA by 2 February 1976—a formal majority of the OAU's member-States, thus obliging the organization to admit the PRA formally to membership on 10 February. The EEC countries granted recognition on 17-18 February, and Portugal followed suit on 22 February. By then, over 70 countries had recognized the MPLA regime.

ECONOMIC AFFAIRS (66.85 Angola escudos = £1 sterling)

While Angola is bound to suffer for some time from the economic scars left by the civil war, there appears little reason to doubt that the country, fabulously wealthy in natural resources, will return in the long-term to its pre-war pattern of rapid economic growth. However, there are several problems to overcome. First, war damage has to be repaired, e.g. the Benguela Railway bridges over the River Kasai, which will have to be rebuilt before Zambian and Zairean copper shipments along the railway can be resumed. Second, Angola now suffers an acute shortage of skilled workers, technicians and administrators following the almost total exodus of the white population. Estimates put the total number of whites remaining in the country

58

by the end of 1975 at 30,000, compared with 700,000 in mid-1974.[91] Few blacks were trained to fill skilled job categories under the colonial regime. In some extreme cases, particularly in small manufacturing concerns, the entire management and skilled workforce fled, forcing the MPLA Government to appoint caretaker administrative committees. This happened, for example, at the *Sociedade Textil de Luanda* (Textang) which was nationalized in October.[92]

PETROLEUM

Angola's pre-war growth pattern was based largely on the country's role as an oil producer.[93] In 1974, Angola produced 8.95 m tons of oil, making Angola the fifth largest oil producer in Africa (after Nigeria, Libya, Algeria and Gabon). In 1975, production dropped to c. 7 m tons—more because of a fall-off in world demand for crude oil than because of Angola's political troubles.[94] Gulf Oil's installations in Cabinda, where over 80% of the country's oil is produced, were not damaged during the war since the MPLA succeeded in maintaining firm control over the enclave throughout the conflict. As the largest oil producer in the country, Gulf pumped 54.6 m barrels from its Cabindan oil-fields in 1974.[95] Gulf's concession area is officially estimated to have reserves of 300 m tons, but unofficial estimates put reserves at over 600 m tons.[96] By mid-1973, Gulf had invested $209 m in Angola and 6% of its world-wide profits and 8-10% of its world-wide production and proved reserves were derived from its Angolan operations.[97] The combined output of the country's four smaller producers (Angol, Petrangol, Texaco and Total) was c. 1.5 m tons a year prior to the war. But Texaco claimed in November 1974 that it had discovered a new offshore field at Santo Antonio do Zaire with reserves ten times larger than those in Cabinda.[98] Oil exports were largely responsible for Angola's soaring trade surplus in recent years and were valued at c. 15,000 m esc (48.8% of total exports) in 1974, compared with 5,755 m esc in 1973, a near-threefold increase due to the rise in world oil prices. As a result, total exports (f.o.b.) nearly doubled from $778 m in 1973 to $1,202 m in 1974; and the trade surplus more than doubled from $236 m to $588 m.[99] Oil is also the basis of the bulk of the Government's revenue. Gulf alone, with annual tax and royalty payments of c. $500 m, provides roughly 60% of the Government's normal revenue.[100] The Government take per barrel set by the Transitional Government during 1975 was 16.67% plus 65.75% tax.[101]

Gulf Oil's Cabindan production and payments to the PRA regime were temporarily suspended in December 1975 following the corporation's receipt of a letter from the US State Department on 19 December. Gulf suspended payment of $125 m due in December 1975 and January 1976 for third quarter taxes and fourth quarter royalties—although it had already paid $116 m to the MPLA-controlled Finance Ministry in Luanda in September. In consequence, Gulf lost $19 m in the last fortnight of December alone.[102] After MPLA's victory, the State Department gave Gulf the green light to resume royalty and tax payments and to open negotiations with the PRA about the resumption of production, which both parties were eager to restart as soon as possible. On 8 March 1976, Gulf turned over its third quarter taxes and fourth quarter royalties to the PRA.[103] MPLA denied any intentions to nationalize Gulf's interests.

MINING

Angola's second most important mining industry, diamonds, was hit harder by the war. Although the mines, concentrated in the north-eastern district of Lunda, were controlled by the MPLA throughout the war, the African labour force dropped during 1975 from 20,000 to 6,000; almost all the industry's skilled white workforce of

2,500 left the country, and productivity had slumped 85% by January 1976. The industry was also affected by an upsurge of illicit diamond mining and smuggling.[104]

Ninety-five per cent of Angola's diamonds are produced by Diamang, a subsidiary of De Beers Consolidated Mines Ltd and the Anglo-American Corporation of SA. The Company has a 50,000-sq. km concession area in the Portugalia region of Lunda. Prior to the war, it was the largest single employer of labour in the country. Like Gulf, the company enjoyed good relations with the MPLA. On 15 January 1976 it was granted a $2 m loan by the PRA regime. Early in 1976, Diamang proposed to the PRA Government that its holdings be nationalized because it was making huge losses (mainly because of the fall in productivity and the rise of illicit diamond mining). Diamang chairman, Carlos Abecassis, said the company wanted to sign a management contract with the Government under which Diamang would continue to run the mines.[105]

Angola's diamond output in 1973 was 2,125,000 carats, with an export value of 1,999 m esc, c. 10% of total exports. Diamonds are the country's third largest foreign exchange earner after oil and coffee. Angola is rich in other minerals, most of which have not yet begun to be exploited: manganese, magnetite, phosphates, gypsum, uranium, asphalt, copper, iron ore, bitumen, alabaster, silica, bauxite, mica, quartz and gold. There are an estimated 23 m tons of copper deposits at Tetelo in Uige, and 80–100 m tons of manganese deposits in Cabinda. Angola is estimated to have iron ore reserves of 130 m tons. Iron ore mining has been centred in Cassinga in southern Angola. Here the *Companhia Mineira de Lòbito* produced c. 6 m tons of iron ore in 1974. All production stopped in August 1975, partly because of the war but also because nearly all the mine's high-grade ore had already been exploited.[106]

AGRICULTURE

The war had a serious effect on Angola's second major export commodity: coffee. Output fell from 3.6 m bags (220,000 tons) in the 1974/5 crop to c. 1-1.5 m bags in the 1975/76 crop, mainly because southerners working in the northern coffee plantations were fearful of FNLA and fled south to Unita strongholds.[107] Short-term supplies of Angolan coffee were not endangered as up to 200,000 tons from previous crops were held in stocks in mid-1975. But the big fall in the 1975/76 Angolan crop, combined with a major setback to the Brazilian crop, threatened to cut sharply into world supply and push up world coffee prices (already £935 a ton in March 1976). Angola normally produces c. three-sixteenths of the world's robusta imports, and in the first nine months of 1974 earned 5,510 m esc of foreign exchange from coffee exports (23.4% of total export earnings).

Other agricultural commodities traditionally exported include sisal (with earnings doubled in 1974 because of the dramatic rise in world prices), cotton, bananas and maize. The country has to import large quantities of wheat. Angola also exported 181,961 tons of wood in 1973. In 1974 it had c. 4.4 m cattle, 2 m goats, 1.29 m pigs and 385,000 sheep. Angola also exports fishmeal and landed 467,000 tons of fish in 1973.[108]

MANUFACTURING

The manufacturing sector is relatively small, contributing c. 17% of GDP. It was severely affected by the war. An inquiry by the Industrial Association of Angola in the Luanda area in October 1975 revealed that 40 of the 150 factories investigated were completely paralyzed because of shortages of essential raw materials and components, lack of electricity, the departure of technicians, managers and workers, and the fall-off in demand for their products.[109] The post-war restoration of communications, coupled with MPLA's drive to raise labour productivity and encourage private investment, were expected to go some way to reviving manufacturing industry. Prior to the war, this sector of·the economy was growing by 19% a year between 1962 and 1971, by 15% in 1972, and by 26.5% in 1973. Investment was c. $50 m a year and manufacturing output stood at 14.1 billion escudos in 1973.[110]

COMMUNICATIONS
The shipment of Zambian and Zairean cargo on the strategic Benguela Railway ground to a standstill in August 1975, when MPLA seized control of the eastern stretch of the line between Luso and Teixeira de Sousa, while Unita took over the central stretch through Bie and Huambo. 140,000 tons of Zambian imports were stranded at Lobito by the railway's closure. Both Zambia and Zaire were forced to suspend exports of copper via Lobito. Zambia had been exporting c. 30,000 tons of copper a month via Lobito (49.7% of its total copper exports in 1974). Zaire exported 200,000 tons of copper and 350,000 tons of manganese via Lobito in 1973. Forty per cent of the railway's revenues are derived from the shipment of international cargo.

BUDGET (in million escudos)

	1969	1970	1971	1973	1974 (forecast)
Ordinary Revenue	7,389	8,767	9,796	13,707	16,442
Extraordinary Revenue	1,999	2,324	2,446	2,623	3,033
Total Expenditure	8,967	10,290	12,079	15,734	19,475
of which: Extraordinary	2,026	2,360	2,446	2,626	4,763
Surplus on Ordinary Budget	421	801	163	596	...

Source: Economist Intelligence Unit, Quarterly Economic Review, Angola and Mozambique, Annual Supplement, 1975.

BALANCE OF PAYMENTS (in million escudos)

	1971	1972	1973
Exports	9,166	12,012	14,475
Imports	11,388	9,310	12,300
Balance on Visible Trade	-2,222	2,702	2,175
Net: Tourism	-512	-193	-741
Transport and Insurance	567	617	1,158
Government Transactions	278	-146	22
Investment Income	-197	-407	-755
Other Services	513	-673	-348
Private Transfers	-310	-225	-228
Balance on Current Account	-1,883	1,675	1,283
Capital Account (net)	70	-709	-982
Total Balance	-1,813	966	301

Source: Economist Intelligence Unit, Quarterly Economic Review, Angola and Mozambique. Annual Supplement, 1975.

ANGOLA'S TRADE (in million escudos)

	1972	1973	1974 (Jan-Sept)
EXPORTS f.o.b.	13,923	19,158	23,557
Coffee	3,835	5,162	5,510
Crude Oil	3,535	5,755	10,789
Diamonds	1,583	1,999	1,731
Iron Ore	1,012	1,210	943
Fishmeal	531	739	374
Sisal	332	462	995
Cotton	284	619	364
Bananas	264	312	231
Maize	143	235	158
IMPORTS c.i.f.	10,728	13,269	11,267
Machinery	2,775	3,037	2,449
Motor Vehicles and Parts	1,310	1,354	847
Iron and Steel	943	1,011	992
Cotton Yarn and Textiles	267	504	—
Medicines	382	474	428
Petroleum Products	390	530	436
Wines	292	304	277
Wheat	142	309	439
Fertilizers	127	202	97
BALANCE	3,195	5,889	12,290

Source: *Economist Intelligence Unit, Quarterly Economic Review, Angola and Mozambique, Annual Supplement, 1975.*

DIRECTION OF ANGOLA'S TRADE (per cent of total values)

	1972	1973	1974 (Jan-Sept)
EXPORTS TO:			
Portugal	26.1	25.2	29.3
Other Overseas Provinces	2.5	2.0	1.5
EEC	12.9	14.1	10.1
Netherlands	3.9	2.5	1.5
West Germany	4.1	5.1	3.3
United Kingdom	3.8	2.8	1.0
US	16.3	28.0	32.7
Japan	10.7	8.8	4.1
Canada	3.9	10.3	14.3
IMPORTS FROM:			
Portugal	23.2	25.4	20.3
Other Overseas Provinces	2.1	2.7	2.4
EEC	37.6	38.1	37.2
West Germany	12.3	13.1	13.2
France	15.9	5.9	6.2
UK	9.0	7.7	7.2
US	12.7	9.6	9.7
Japan	5.7	5.6	4.5
South Africa	4.6	5.8	11.0

Source: *Economist Intelligence Unit, Quarterly Economic Review, Angola and Mozambique, Annual Supplement, 1975.*

NOTES

1. See *Africa Contemporary Record (ACR)* 1974-5, pp. 221-6.
2. See *ACR* 1972-3, p. B477.
3. For a fuller discussion see essay in *ACR* 1975-6, *A Study of International Involvement in Angola.*
4. *Jornal Novo*, 5 September 1975; *Angola Report*, 16 May 1975.
5. *Africa Research Bulletin*, Vol. 12, No. 7, 15 August 1975.
6. *Portuguese Africa* 28 February 1975.
7. See essay in *ACR* 1975-6 on *Portugal's Year in Africa.*
8. For a fuller discussion see essay in *ACR* 1975-6 on *A Study of International Involvement in Angola.*
9. *Afriscope*, August 1975.
10. See *ACR* 1974-5, p. B333; B528. B533; B536-7; B538; C56.
11. *The Guardian*, Manchester, 15 February 1975.
12. *Zambia Daily Mail*, 22 February 1975.
13. *O Seculo*, 24 March 1975.
14. *To The Point International*, 22 February 1975.
15. *Radio Luanda*, 2 February 1975.
16. *Economist Intelligence Unit*, Quarterly Economic Review, Angola and Mozambique, 1st Quarter, 1975.
17. See *ACR* 1974-5, p. B530.
18. Johannesburg *Star Weekly*, 5 April 1975.
19. *Radio Luanda*, 30 March 1975.
20. *Frankfurter Allgemeine Zeitung*, 29 March 1975.
21. *Le Monde*, 10 April 1975.
22. *The Guardian*, 5 May 1975.
23. *Le Monde*, 10 May 1975.
24. *Angola Report*, 23 May 1975.
25. *The Guardian*, 6 June 1975.
26. *United Press International*, 6 June 1975.
27. *A Provincia de Angola*, 8 June 1975.
28. *United Press International*, 9 June 1975.
29. *Agence France Presse*, 12 June 1975.
30. *Agence France Presse*, 8 June 1975.
31. See *Angola: A Failure of African Policy.*
32. See Documents Section under Political Issues in *ACR* 1975-6.
33. *The Times*, London, 12 May 1975.
34. See Documents Section under Political Issues in *ACR* 1975-6.
35. *Ibid* for leaders' explanations of reasons for breakdown.
36. *Financial Times*, 3 July 1975.
37. *Lisbon Radio*, 6 July 1975.
38. *Luanda Radio*, 4 July 1975.
39. *Luanda Radio*, 6 July 1975.
40. *Luanda Radio*, 12 July 1975.
41. *The Observer*, 27 July 1975.
42. *New York Times*, 25 September 1975; see also essay in this volume on Foreign Intervention in Angola.
43. *Diario de Noticias*, 15 July 1975.
44. *The Observer*, 27 July 1975.
45. *Agence France Presse*, 25 July 1975.
46. *Agence France Presse*, 25 July 1975.
47. *Agence France Presse*, 29 July 1975.
48. *The Observer*, 27 July 1975.
49. *Daily Telegraph*, 26 July 1975.
50. *Diario de Noticias*, 21 May 1975; *Le Soir*, 14 July 1975.
51. *O Seculo*, 23 May 1975.
52. *Zambia Daily Mail*, 6 November 1975.
53. *The Times*, 18 July 1975; see also essay in this volume on *Portugal's Year in Africa.*
54. *Diario de Noticias*, 16 May 1975.
55. *The Guardian*, 17 May 1975.
56. *Financial Times*, 9 June 1975.
57. *Le Monde*, 25 September 1975; *Jornal Novo*, 2 October 1975; *Star Weekly*, 11 October 1975.
58. *The Guardian*, 29 October 1975.

59. See *ACR* 1974-5, p. 532 ff.
60. *New York Times*, 11 November 1975; *Jornal Novo*, 12 November 1975; *Le Monde*, 13 November 1975.
61. See Note 3.
62. *The Guardian*, Manchester, 29 September 1975.
63. Lourenco Marques *Noticias*, 15 August 1975.
64. *The Times*, London, 15 December 1975; *The Guardian*, Manchester, 18 December 1975.
65. *Southern Africa*, December 1975.
66. See Note 3.
67. For a detailed account of the Cunene River scheme, see *African Development*, November 1975.
68. *The Observer*, 16 November 1975.
69. *Ibid* 27 October 1975.
70. *Ibid* 16 November 1975.
71. For Neto's Independence Day speech see Documents Section under Political Issues in *ACR* 1975-6.
72. For Roberto's Proclamation of Independence see Documents Section under Political Issues in *ACR* 1975-6.
73. For Kinshasa Agreement see Documents Section under Political Issues in *ACR* 1975-6.
74. See Note 3. Also essay in *ACR* 1975-6 on *The OAU's Year in Africa*.
75. See Documents Section under Political Issues in *ACR* 1975-6.
76. *Lagos Radio*, 27 November 1975.
77. For Lourenco Marcques Declaration see Documents Section, Political Issues in *ACR* 1975-6.
78. See Note 3, and essay in *ACR* 1975-6 on *The OAU's Year in Africa*.
79. *Financial Times*, 30 December 1975.
80. *Ibid* 2 January 1976.
81. *Tanjug*, 13 January 1976; *Financial Times*, 14 January 1976.
82. *El Moudjahid*, 15 November 1975.
83. *Marches Tropicaux*, 5 December 1975.
84. *International Herald Tribune*, 13 December 1975.
85. *The Guardian*, Manchester, 21 January 1976.
86. See Note 3.
87. *AZAP*, 20 November 1975.
88. *The Times*, London, 11 December 1975.
89. *Ibid* 16 December 1975.
90. *Radio Johannesburg*, 4 February 1976.
91. *Economist Intelligence Unit* (EIU) Quarterly Economic Review, Angola and Mozambique, Fourth Quarter, 1975.
92. *Marches Tropicaux*, 10 October 1975.
93. See *ACR* 1974-5, p. B541.
94. *Petroleum Economist*, January 1976.
95. *Portuguese Africa*, 10 January 1975.
96. *Sunday Times*, 24 March 1974.
97. *EIU*, Quarterly Economic Review, Angola and Mozambique, Annual Supplement, 1975.
98. Johannesburg *Star*, 11 November 1974.
99. *UN Monthly Bulletin of Statistics*, December 1975; *The Times*, 2 February 1976.
100. *The Guardian*, 22 December 1975.
101. *Jornal de Angola*, 19 August 1975.
102. *The Guardian*, 22 December 1975; *Financial Times*, 20 February 1976.
103. *Radio Luanda*, 10 March 1976.
104. *International Herald Tribune*, 7 October 1975; *The Times*, 24 February 1976.
105. *The Times*, 24 February 1976.
106. *EIU*, Quarterly Economic Review, Angola and Mozambique, Annual Supplement, 1975.
107. *The Guardian*, 23 February 1976; *EIU*, Quarterly Economic Review, Angola and Mozambique, 3rd Quarter, 1975.
108. *EIU*, Quarterly Economic Review, Angola and Mozambique, Annual Supplement, 1975.
109. *Marches Tropicaux*, 7 November 1975.
110. *EIU*, Quarterly Economic Review, Angola and Mozambique, Annual Supplement, 1975.

PART FOUR

DOCUMENTS

ANGOLA
OAU Resolution on the Situation in Angola

12th Ordinary Session of the Assembly of Heads of
State and Government, Kampala, Uganda,
28 July-1 August 1975
AHG/Res. 72 (XII)

The Assembly of Heads of State and Government of the OAU, Having noted Resolution CM/Res. 424 (XXV) on the situation in Angola, Having heard the Statements of the representatives of the MPLA, FNLA and Unita and of the Acting Prime Minister of the Transitional Government of Angola on the situation in this territory, Deploring the bloody confrontations between the principal Liberation Movements and the non-respect by the signatories of the Agreements of Kinshasa, Mombasa, Alvor and Nakuru:

1. Urgently appeals to all Liberation Movements to lay down their arms;
2. Earnestly requests Portugal to assume, without delay and in an impartial manner, its responsibilities in Angola;
3. Decides to send a Fact-Finding Commission of Enquiry and Conciliation to Angola immediately;
4. Requests the Current Chairman of OAU, after consultation with Members of the Bureau, to appoint members of the Fact-Finding Commission of Enquiry and Conciliation;
5. Requests the OAU Defence Commission, assisted by the OAU Secretary-General, following the Report of the Commission of Enquiry, to consider the necessity of creating and despatching an OAU Peace Force to Angola and to submit its recommendations to the Council of Ministers.
6. Calls upon Liberation Movements, the Transitional Angolan Government, the Portuguese Government and neighbouring countries to co-operate with the OAU Fact-Finding Commission of Enquiry and Conciliation.

The Mombasa Agreements, January 1975

OAU Council of Ministers, Kampala, 18-25 October 1975

Declaration of Principles (FNLA, MPLA, Unita)

The three Angolan Liberation Movements (FNLA, MPLA and Unita) meeting in Mombasa, Republic of Kenya from the 3 to 5 January 1975 seriously analyzed and reviewed with concern the present political situation in Angola at this stage of decolonization. Considering that the summit conference for the constitutional talks between the three Angolan liberation movements and the Portuguese Government will be held in Portugal on the 10 January 1975; considering that the above referred conference will lead to the formation of a Transitional Government and consequently to national independence; the delegations of FNLA, MPLA and Unita have adopted and agreed on the following common declaration of principles:

1. **On Territorial Integrity:** The three liberation movements have reiterated their determination to safeguard the territorial integrity of Angola within its present geographical and administrative boundaries. It is within this context that Cabinda is considered to be an integral and inalienable part of Angola.
2. **On National Unity:** The delegations of FNLA, MPLA and Unita are fully committed to forge and build a just and democratic society in Angola, thus eliminate ethnic, racial and religious discrimination and all other forms of discrimination.

3. On Economic Situation: Similarly, the three liberation movements are deeply concerned with the deterioration of the economic situation of Angola. The movements urge the Portuguese Government to take immediate and effective measures which will safeguard the social interests of the workers, and stimulate the economic development and the process of national reconstruction of the country.

FINAL COMMUNIQUE
The delegations of FNLA, MPLA and Unita led by their respective Presidents, Mr Holden Roberto, Dr Agostinho Neto and Dr Jonas Savimbi met at State House, Mombasa, Republic of Kenya from 3 to 5 January 1975, thanks to the goodwill and availability of the Government of the Republic of Kenya.

The meeting evolved in an atmosphere of mutual and perfect understanding. As a result, the delegations found a common political platform in the light of the negotiations with the Portuguese Government for the formation of a transitional Government which will lead Angola to independence. The three delegations analyzed all problems related to the decolonization process and to the future sovereign State of Angola.

The delegation agreed on a common political platform which includes, among other questions, those related to the formation of the Transitional Government, to the question of the armed forces in Angola and to the creation and instalation of future institutions.

Within the same spirit of understanding and unity, the three Liberation Movements decided that, from now on, they will co-operate in all spheres and especially in that of decolonization for the defence of the territorial integrity as well as for the national reconstruction. Consequently, the three liberation movements declare, as of today, their readiness to initiate immediate negotiations with the Portuguese Government at a summit conference to be held in Portugal at the proposed date.

Finally, FNLA, MPLA and Unita express their sincere and fraternal gratitude to the President Mzee Jomo Kenyatta, to the Government and the people of Kenya for the excellent hospitality extended.

Joint Communique between MPLA and FNLA

The delegations of MPLA and FNLA, meeting in Mombasa during the meeting of the three Angolan liberation movements, have analyzed the present situation of the country and established a basis of co-operation with a view to avoid further deterioration in the relationship between the two movements at this stage of decolonization; bearing in mind that the unity of the Angolan liberation movements is essential in the struggle against colonialism and an instrument to safeguard and consolidate national independence; cognizant of the fact that the interference of foreign interests in the national political life, and that the existence of reactionary forces in Angola are a threat to independence and harmonious development of the Angolan society; deeply concerned with the deteriorating economic and social conditions of the Angolan people and with the economic situation of the country; agree to:

1. End all types of hostilities and propaganda which may impede frank and sincere collaboration between MPLA and FNLA.

2. Create a favourable climate of close co-operation and mutual respect between the two movements from top to bottom and in all spheres.

3. To constantly defend the interests of the Angolan people, especially those of the most exploited ones, and jointly struggle for the extinction of all remnants of colonialism.

4. To co-operate in common organs for the solution of problems of the very people.

5. Not to interfere in the internal affairs of the signatories of this agreement.

6. To oppose by all means any manoeuvres of reactionary forces aimed at

perpetuating unjust relations inherited from colonialism, thus struggling against all manoeuvres which jeopardize national unity and aimed at secession of any part of our country.

President of MPLA: Dr Agostinho Neto; President of FNLA: Holden Roberto; State House Mombasa, 5 January 1975.

For the Alvor Agreement between Portugal and the MPLA/FNLA/Unita see *Africa Contemporary Record* 1974-5, pp. 221ff.

The Nakuru Agreement, 16–21 June 1975

The Angolan liberation movements, the National Front for the Liberation of Angola (FNLA), the People's Movement for the Liberation of Angola (MPLA), and the National Union for the Total Independence of Angola (Unita) meeting in Nakuru from 16 to 21 June 1975, and represented by their respective Presidents, Holden Roberto, Agostinho Neto and Jonas Savimbi, aware of the gravity of the situation prevailing in the country, and that national interests must be made to prevail over any political and ideological divergences, solemnly pledge to renounce the use of force as a means of solving problems and to honour all commitments deriving from the conclusions reached in the accord as hereinafter mentioned:

Article One. An appraisal of the overall situation in Angola and of the relations between the national liberation movements.

Taking stock of the overall situation in the country, the Angolan liberation movements, FNLA, MPLA and Unita, with great concern, state that the following factors have contributed to the deterioration of that situation in Angola.

(1) The introduction [into the country] by the liberation movements of large quantities of arms, following the 25 April [coup in Portugal] and especially after the movements' establishment in Luanda. This arms race is attributable to the fact that the liberation movements have continued to hold a mutual mistrust, stemming from their political and ideological differences and past divergences.

(2) The absence of political tolerance, revealed in the violence resorted to in the pattern of activity of the liberation movements and their militants.

(3) The existence of the so-called strongholds (zonas de influencia) and of areas of a supposed military superiority.

(4) The arming of civilians.

(5) Clashes between the troops of the liberation movements and the tendency of the latter to regionalize their forces which, apart from causing harm to numerous innocent victims, aggravates the situation by leading to the spreading of tribalism, regionalism and racism.

(6) The presence of reactionary agitation and of elements alien to the process of decolonization.

In the face of such situation and with a view to restoring a climate of peace in Angola, the FNLA, the MPLA and Unita have decided:

(1) To induce a climate of political tolerance and national unity within Angola's political and ideological diversity.

(2) Solemnly to undertake to put an end to all forms of violence and intimidation of militants, and immediately to set free all prisoners held by each other.

(3) To safeguard all liberation movements' right to freely exercise political activity in any part of the country.

(4) To speed up the formation of a national army.

(5) To disarm civilians, after establishing the necessary conditions.

(6) To speed up the deportation of the former agents of PIDE-DGS still in Angola.

(7) To take measures to curb internal and external reactionary forces.

(8) To call upon the information departments of the Government and of the liberation movements to help publicize the aforementioned measures.

Article Two. The performance of the Transitional Government.

The Angola liberation movements, FNLA, MPLA and Unita, after reviewing the performance of the Transitional Government are of the opinion: that the Transitional Government has made laudable efforts towards resolving the problems besetting the nation: however, in the performance of its duties, the Government has encountered difficulties placed in its way by the liberation movements, either because of their acting in disregard of the decisions of the Government, or by failure to give it the support necessary for it to be able to execute such decisions, that hitherto the Government was unable to exercise its authority nor fully to assume its responsibilities, that the situation is aggravated by the absence of proper political and military machinery capable of safeguarding the security of the State and, at the same time, enforcing measures to ensure compliance with the law.

The inconstancy of justice, the liberation movements practice of summary justice and their shielding of militants committing illegal acts have also contributed to the impairing of Government's authority. Moreover, the people of Angola are not sufficiently informed of the Government's efforts. On the contrary, they find themselves in situations which place them in conflict with the Government because of the lack of intermediary organs acting as a direct bridge between the Government and the people. Furthermore, a number of both senior and junior employees in certain Ministries are deeply affected by party politics and turn their Ministries into fiefdoms owing exclusive allegiance to the Movement to which their Minister belongs.

Mention must also be made of some aspects of individual performance of Ministers: (a) their lack of responsibility; (b) their visits to places outside Luanda and abroad, without the approval of the Transitional Government; (c) their failure to implement the decisions taken by the Council of Ministers; (d) the elaboration and execution of plans without consulting and obtaining the agreement of the Council of Ministers; and their difficulty while in government service in distinguishing their affiliation to a liberation movement and their position as members of the Government.

Again, the disturbances of public order, characterized by armed clashes between liberation movements, has greatly contributed to the deterioration of the situation.

Also noted was the arrogation by the National Defence Commission and the Presidential Council to themselves of responsibilities for solutions to problems falling within the competence of the Council of Ministers and/or individual Ministries, as well as the question of the impartiality of the Press and radio.

Therefore, in a bid to find solutions to the problems which prevent the Transitional Government from functioning properly in this crucial phase of the decolonization process, the Angola liberation movements, the FNLA, the MPLA and Unita have decided:

To strengthen the hands of the Government and to see to it that militants at all levels comply with the decisions of the Government; to co-operate positively with the Government in the enforcement of measures taken, in all spheres of national life, political, economic and military; to refrain from arrogating to themselves Government prerogatives, which belong to it alone; to co-operate actively with the Government in producing a blueprint for a common political, economic and social programme, embodying the principles of all the liberation movements;

To institute without delay, in conjunction with the quarters concerned, subordinate organs of sovereignty that will execute, control and guarantee the proper functioning of the Government, such as national armed forces and departmental police forces, for instance the mining and border police; to demand from the Government a reorganization of the judicial machine, designed to put an end to justice by private trials; to encourage the people's participation in the affairs of the nation through people's organizations set up by the liberation movements, at ward, village, farm, office, workshop, school and other grassroot levels, by making of the administrative and trade union machinery; to discourage and combat party favouritism within the departments of Ministries; to demand that the Government fully applies its code of discipline and introduces a set of rules which would enable it to reprimand and/or issue a vote of no confidence as a means of punishing those committing serious mistakes;

To demand that the Presidential Council and the National Defence Commission act within the bounds of the prerogatives and powers conferred upon them by the law in force; to demand that the Ministries carry out the decisions so far taken by the Council of Ministers; to demand that the Government adopt austerity measures in the sectors of the economy and finance; to call on the workers and contractors fully to exploit the capacity of the production means available in the country; not to hinder the free movement of persons and goods throughout the national territory; to demand that the Government appoints a committee of inquiry to detect the former agents of the PIDE-DGS and colonialists notorious for their fascist practices and all those who played a part in the massacre of people, with the aim of speeding up their deportation from the country. At the same time, the agents and informers of Angolan nationality must be rounded up, brought to court and punished or rehabilitated.

The conference accepted the fact that there were civilians equipped with arms given to them by the three liberation movements, for reasons known to history, in the course of their armed struggle for liberation and, later, to enable them to fight the reactionary forces. It was, however, observed that this problem must now be resolved because, as everyone knows full well, civilians are difficult to control once they are armed. This fact poses a threat to peace in Angola and inflames tribal dissensions. The conference also took into account that these armed civilians must be called upon to give up their arms voluntarily, in order that the security of the inhabitants of Angola shall be safeguarded. It [the conference] accordingly came to the conclusions:

(1) That there is a need to put an effective and immediate stop to attacks and acts of retaliation by the liberation movements against each ôther and against civilians, and that disputes between the liberation movements or between them and civilians must be settled by discussion.

(2) That the liberation movements should launch an all-out campaign designed to impress upon armed civilians the importance, both politically as well as morally, of giving up their arms and, at the same time, the evils of tribalism, regionalism and racism.

(3) That such a campaign be compulsorily assisted by all news media, be they public or privately-owned.

(4) That the Presidential Council appoint a committee in each of the country's districts, directly responsible to the Council and made up of representatives of all three liberation movements, vested with responsiblity to: (a) collate all data on armed civilians; (b) seek out and disarm any elements of reactionary forces; and (c) assist in the campaign designed to enlighten the public on the question of disarming civilians.

(5) That such disarmament committees submit the results of their operations to the Presidential Council which, in turn, will take appropriate action to take over the custody of such recovered arms, through the National Defence Commission.

(6) That the Ministry of Justice drafts legislation designed to mete out severe punishment to those infringing the aforesaid measures.

Article Four [as numbered]—The disarming of Zambians and the former Katangese Gendarmes.

The summit meeting of the Angola liberation movements, FNLA, MPLA and Unita, after analyzing the existence in Angola of Zambians and former Katangese gendarmes equipped with arms, and recognizing that the precence of such armed foreigners can pose a threat to the peace and security of the nation, decided:

(1) To reassert the provisions of the Alvor Accord relevant to the need immediately to disarm the former Katangese gendarmes and Zambians living in Angola.

(2) To impress upon neighbouring countries to act likewise with regard to Angolans living in those countries engaged in condemnable political activities

detrimental to the interests of the Angolan people and which are a threat to Angola's territorial integrity and constitute a flagrant interference with our country's internal affairs.

Resolution on Cabinda. The summit meeting of the Angola liberation movements, after making an appraisal of the overall situation in the country and mindful of the principles of unity and territorial integrity spelt out in Article Three of the Alvor Accord, and of those enshrined in the Charters of the OAU and the UN:

(1) Reasserts that Angola's geographical and political boundaries remain as they have previously existed and, as such, Cabinda is an integral and inseparable part of its territory.

(2) Directs the Transitional Government to clarify and defend this position at international bodies whenever it is deemed necessary.

Article Five—The appointment of organs of sovereignty and the creation of national armed forces.

The Angola liberation movements, FNLA, MPLA and Unita, recognizing the need to create an instrument that is capable of protecting the country's territorial integrity and of maintaining peace and order in Angola, and in view of the inefficiency of the mixed military forces created under the terms of the Alvor Accord, and, further, recognizing the fact that the structural and functional pattern of the military mixed forces, far from paving the way for the formation of a true Angolan national army have only encouraged party divisions, have accordingly decided:

(1) On the need to set up the national armed forces of Angola, to assist fully towards the creation of such national forces, and to provide the required military complements:

First, that a permanent military commission be appointed with this in view, made up of a senior officer from each of the liberation movements, totalling three such officers, and responsible to the Presidential Council of the Transitional Government, invested with the following responsibilities, in addition to those the Council may deem necessary to assign: (a) to prepare the necessary material and technical conditions for setting up the national armed forces; (b) to draw up constitutional foundations for such national armed forces; (c) to list the material and manpower resources available to such national armed forces; (d) to provide the Presidential Council with an estimate of funds necessary for the upkeep of such national armed forces; (e) to determine the location where such national armed forces should establish their trading centres; (f) to outline the patriotic foundations that will govern national armed forces and orientate their members in the framework of national unity, defence of territorial integrity, peace and defence of democratic rule; (g) to appoint the appropriate organs required to carry out the measures laid down above.

Secondly, that the strength of such national armed forces should not exceed a maximum of 30,000 men and that their integration will be gradual, at whatever pace the commission shall lay down.

Thirdly, that the permanent military commission be given the task of demobilizing troops surplus to the strength laid down and also of stipulating the time limit within which the first units of the national armed forces of Angola shall be formed.

(2) To demand that the National Defence Commission step up the process of integration of mixed military forces by:

Firstly, closing down the liberation movements' individual training camps and setting up common training camps for the Angolan members of the mixed military forces.

Secondly, laying down a standard code of discipline and a common and uniform system of ranks.

Thirdly, abolishing emblems and insignia, such as berets, boots, uniforms, belts and anything else which is indicative of the servicemen's affiliation to any particular movement, and introducing one single uniform and set of emblems.

Article Six—The transfer of power and elections.

Reiterating the principles solemnly affirmed in the Alvor Accord, the Angola liberation movements, the FNLA, the MPLA and Unita are still of the view that in Angola the most adequate way of ensuring a peaceful transfer of power, leading to independence, is by elections.

In view of the fact that the atmosphere which prevailed following the Transitional Government's taking office made it difficult for the Government to promulgate the Portuguese constitutional (fundamental) law and the electoral law within the time limit stipulated in the Alvor Accord, the conference recognized that a climate of peace and ideological tolerance among the people and between the liberation movements is a prerequisite for the electoral process. It is clearly necessary therefore for the national army, that will be the guarantor of peace and democracy and the protector of internal and external security, to be set up without further delay.

Because of the shortage of time between now and 11 November and the complexity of the electoral process, the liberation movements undertake to make every effort towards holding elections. However, should difficulties arise in this respect, they would consider an alternative course. To this end, the liberation movements decided:

(1) That the Transitional Government immediately make available to the (electoral) commission all material means designed to assist it in its task of formulating the projected electoral law by 5 July 1975.

(2) That the Council of Ministers should resume its debate on the electoral law, so as to enable its promulgation by 15 July 1975.

(3) That soon after the electoral law is promulgated a. body should be established to organize the electoral processes.

(4) That the Transitional Government, through the Ministry of Planning and Finance, survey the material and financial implications of the electoral process, taking into account the funds that will have to be provided to the liberation movements towards their electioneering campaigns.

(5) To propose the following dates and time limits for the main items of the electoral process: (a) registration of voters to be completed within a minimum of 60 days from 1 August 1975; (b) a minimum of 20 days for the electoral campaign; (c) the election itself to be held on a date within the month of October 1975; and (d) that the constituent assembly should hold its first meeting on a date in early November 1975.

(6) That, should difficulties arise in implementing this timetable, a fresh summit meeting will be held in Angola, to devise an alternative formula for the transfer of power.

(7) That the necessary amendments be made to the relevant provisions of the draft constitutional law arising from these points.

Article Seven— The problem of refugees and displaced persons.

The Angola liberation movements, the FNLA, MPLA and Unita, in view of the fact that hundreds of thousands of Angolan refugees are now making their way back to their homeland following the end of the armed struggle and as the reasons which led to their flight no longer exist; alive to the need to provide relief for them and to organize their immediate rehabilitation before reintegration into the economic and social life of the nation; and mindful of the need to implement the provision of the Alvor Accord relating to the setting up of a national refugee committee—which has not yet been done despite the fact that the situation warrants such action—have decided:

(1)' To formalize the appointment of the national refugee committee, endowing it with an efficient functional organization.

(2) That the National Refugee Committee should step up its work so as to be able: (a) to draw up and submit for Government approval plans to be submitted to international bodies aimed at securing relief aid for the refugees and displaced persons; (b) to establish the principle for giving priority to those who became refugees as a result of the struggle for national independence; (c) to devise a plan designed to provide full assistance to the refugees and displaced persons by creating conditions that will promote their economic and social advancement; (d) in conjunction with the Ministry of the Interior, to control the re-entry of such refugees by setting up special reception centres at the places of entry.

(3) That the Transitional Government should approach the governments of countries bordering on Angola with a view to enlisting their help in facilitating the

return of the refugees.

(4) That the Ministry of Health and Social Services should co-ordinate the activies of the national refugee committee, paying due regard to its functions and not assuming such functions itself.

(5) To call on international bodies to provide urgent assistance to enable the Transitional Government of Angola to carry out this task.

Article Eight—The Department of Foreign Affairs.

The Angola liberation movements, the FNLA, the MPLA and Unita, aware of the need for Angola to begin contacts with foreign countries and that it is up to the Presidential Council actively to pursue the question of Angola's external relations, have reached agreement that a Department of Foreign Relations be set up immediately, of heterogeneous composition, connection with and responsible for promoting, in conjunction with the High Commissioner, the policies of Angola's external relations.

Article Nine—The economic and financial situation.

The Angola liberation movements, FNLA, MPLA and Unita, assessing the economic and financial situation of the country, noted:

(1) A worsening of the crisis inherited from the colonial regime, especially in the industrial and rural economy sectors.

(2) A deterioration of the public finances, balance of trade and external credits.

(3) An absence of guidelines and of co-ordination of a uniform external trade policy.

(4) A systematic paralysis in the country's main seaports, a factor which, coupled with the already worsening situation brought about by low production, has badly hit the import and export trade indispensable to the country's economic growth and the welfare of her inhabitants.

(5) A climate of insecurity, which is mainly responsible for the continuing exodus of skilled personnel whose presence in Angola is regarded as being of paramount importance.

(6) Systematic strikes of workers without prior approval by their respective unions, together with demands for higher wages which, in the face of current economic resources of the country, cause a drop in national productivity and further inflationary trends, whose effects hit the working classes hardest.

(7) A marked increase in the smuggling of diamonds, which has a negative effect on the balance of payments and public finances, causing upsets in the international markets.

(8) The absence of effective controls at the borders as a factor facilitating the ilicit import and export of goods.

(9) The shortage of supplies at various population centres in the country, particularly in Luanda, brought about by the state of insecurity and due to barriers being placed on the roads leading to and from the capital.

Therefore, considering that these difficulties arise partly because of the absence of co-ordination between the liberation movements and the Transitional Government, and partly because of the state of tension and crisis by armed clashes, it has been decided:

(1) That urgent and firm steps be taken by the Transitional Government to speed up clearance of the ports of Luanda and Lobito and to end the standstill there.

(2) That trade agreements should be compulsorily submitted for the approval of the Council of Ministers before they are concluded.

(3) That the Transitional Government should take firm action against technocrats and businessmen whose activities are regarded as attempts to sabotage the economic development of the country.

(4) That the Transitional Government should take firm and effective measures to prevent strikes or wage demands which jeopardize the economic stability of the country.

(5) That the Transitiona Government should define and instigate a wages policy and a policy of equal pay for equal work, suited to local conditions.

(6) That the Transitional Government should instigate a policy designed to control inflation and should adopt stern measures to curb speculation and hoarding.

(7) That the diamond-mining areas should be declared military zones and military and police patrols immediately reinforced there speedily to expose all persons or groups illicitly trafficking in diamonds.

(8) That the Transitional Government should strengthen the number of policemen manning the border posts.

(9) That the Transitional Government should approve the appointment of the committees provided for in Article 56 of the Alvor Accord.

(10) That all barriers placed on communication routes or main roads leading to and from urban centres, particularly in and around Luanda, should be removed without delay and that troops should be stationed at all main access roads from and to urban centres, particularly in and around Luanda, providing efficient protection for the free movement of persons and goods.

(11) To support the Transitional Government by assuring it of the means necessary to put all decisions included in this agreement into practice.

[Dated:] Nakuru, 21st June 1975. [Signed:] Holden Roberto for FNLA, Agostinho Neto for MPLA, Jonas Savimbi for Unita.

Reasons given for breakdown of agreements and relations with OAU

Statement of the MPLA Political Bureau read over Luanda Radio by its President, Dr Agostinho Neto, on 16 July 1975

The Political Bureau of the MPLA has once again examined the delicate situation we are now living through in the country, particularly in the towns of Luanda and Dalatando. Thorough analysis of the events shows clearly that, like the experience of what already happened in relation to the Mombasa and Alvor Agreements, the FNLA has systematically violated the Nakuru Agreement, continuing in practice a policy of intimidation of the population and armed operations against positions occupied by the MPLA. Very much in evidence are the recent assaults on homes and the arrest, torture and murder of MPLA sympathizers, the recent armed action against the villages of Tangu and Kassumba and Kambaya, as well as the outrageous shooting attack on the procession accompanying the funeral of a militant of the Organization of Angola Women, which unleashed the present disturbances in Luanda.

These systematic actions which yet again expose the use of violence by the FNLA in order to take power, are aimed at creating situations which disrupt the people's normal life, because FAPLA (the MPLA forces) has always tried to answer only with purely defensive action. Experience has shown, however, that regardless of other factors, the imposed presence of the forces of ELNA (FNLA forces) among the people and the outrages committed by those forces constitutes one of the fundamental causes supplementing clashes and provocation which rapidly degenerate into armed conflicts.

The MPLA continues to note, in statements by the spokesman of the Portuguese side, both within the National Defence Commission and outside it, the lack of proper care either as regards the appreciation of the events or in the timeliness of such appreciation. Indeed, the National Defence Commission has never dealt thoroughly with the occupation of the north-west of Angola by the FNLA, nor with the extent of the outrages committed there, or the real origins of the continuing deterioration of the situation in Luanda and other parts of the country, almost always reverting to a strange silence which is practically only broken when it is a matter of accusing the MPLA.

Furthermore, the communique of 12 July signed by the High Commissioner of the Portuguese Republic in Angola, Unita and the FNLA, in the name of the National Defence Commission, does not in any way reflect reality, deliberately ignoring yet again the successive violations practised by the FNLA which have led to the present confrontations, the spread of which they want to blame on the MPLA, which has always reacted by maintaining a defensive attitude.

Thus, denying the right of the National Defence Commission to take decisions in the absence of one of its constituent parts, the MPLA categorically rejects both the terms and content of the communique of 12 July signed by the High Commissioner, General Silva Cardoso, Unita and the FNLA.

Convinced of the need to respect the Alvor and Nakuru Agreements, the MPLA is of the opinion that only if the FNLA seeks to withdraw its forces from Luanda, the excess troops of ELNA, and guarantees the cessation of outrages against the people in their homes, in the streets and at places of work, will it be possible to restore normal life and peace.

The MPLA is continuing always to study and put into effect measures guaranteeing the correct implementation of the Alvor and Nakuru Agreements.

Throughout the whole of the agitated period of the events referred to above, with perfect co-ordination between the Central Committee, the Political Bureau and the General Staff of FAPLA, the Political Bureau has urged the brave FAPLA fighters, all militants and sympathizers, and also CMA (Organization of Angola Women), the JMPLA (MPLA Youth), OPA (Organization of Angolan Pioneers) and UNTA (National Union of Angolan Workers), always to act in collaboration with the leading bodies, making every effort to avoid even greater suffering for the civilian population. The struggle continues! Victory is certain!

Statement by Political Bureau of the MPLA
Luanda, 29 September 1975

Being a country of inexhaustible economic potentialities, Angola has been one of the primary targets of imperialist greed on the African continent. Consequently, various kinds of foreign interference has been a constant of Angolan life, and it is not surprising, therefore, that a puppet Angolan party emerged to defend those foreign interests under the guise of a liberation movement. Furthermore, this party was born on foreign soil,.first under the name of Union of the Peoples of Northern Angola, UPNA, and later as Union of the Peoples of Angola, UPA. But, in the face of the victorious offensive of the Angolan people under the direction of the MPLA, imperialism adopted the strategy of splitting the strongly tribalized UPA grouping into other parties, also regionalized, but with leanings towards other areas of the country. Thus there emerged FLEC for Cabinda and Unita for the centre of the country.

This UPA-FNLA-Unita-FLEC combine is, in fact, composed of tribal groupings bent on provoking the division of the country into parts enslaved by foreign interests. This combine cannot, therefore, be regarded as a liberation movement and it is in this context that must be viewed the political and military intervention by Zaire, which plays the role of a springboard for the financing, equipping, supplying with arms and assembly of these puppet groupings. The presence of Zairean troops in Angola has been fully proved at a Press conference in Luanda when a number of elements of the invading army were displayed to the news media, together with some Portuguese mercenaries recruited from Rhodesia; and at this precise moment, SA troops continue to occupy parts of Angolan territory.

All this reveals that a large scale imperialist plan to stifle the Angolan people and the MPLA is systematically being put into effect, relying on the domestic front on tribal groupings and on the external front in Zaire in the north and SA in the south. With the intent of concealing or justifying such a plan, the imperialists and their lackeys have gone to the ridiculous extreme of declaring that Mozambican, Zambian, Cuban, Russian, Guinean, Czechoslovak and Yugoslav mercenaries were fighting in the ranks of the MPLA.

Our history has throughout shown how much the MPLA has respected the OAU and abided by its decisions. For this reason, the MPLA is profoundly surprised by the fact that this has not been reciprocated, in that a move has just been initiated concerning Angola, led by the chairman of the OAU, about which the MPLA, Angola's only liberation movement, has not been consulted once.

It is in this order of things that on 23rd of this month, there took place in Kinshasa a meeting between the chairman of the OAU, the President of the Republic of Zaire and leaders of Unita and FNLA, as a result of which a meeting on Angola appears to have been convened in Kampala on 30th of this month, about which the only details MPLA has are those supplied by the Press. The MPLA, therefore, draws the OAU's attention to the decisions due to be taken at that Kampala meeting and reaffirms that the Angolan problems should only be resolved by the Angolan people themselves. The MPLA is ready to explain to the OAU, at any time, its view of the Angolan problem. The fight goes on; victory is certain.

Statement by Dr Agostinho Neto on 1 October 1975

Our enemies, the imperialists and their lackeys, persist in conspiring against the interests of our people, especially against the interests of the more exploited strata of our masses. The imperialists, as our comrades are aware, have once again taken it upon themselves to organize a conciliation meeting today, in the Ugandan capital of Kampala, at which also we, the MPLA, were supposed to be present, in order to be reconciled with Unita and FNLA. As you are aware, the MPLA made its position public long ago. We do not regard Unita or FNLA as liberation movements. We regard them as invading forces, at the service of imperialism, with whom we no longer have anything to talk about. We, the MPLA, hold that the only liberation movement in Angola is the MPLA. And for this reason we do not have to sit again at the negotiating table with Unita and FNLA.

Mark you, last night, Senhor General [sic] telephoned me and asked me to be present in Kampala today. We have a deep respect for the OAU, and General Amin is the chairman of OAU. Neither as a movement nor in the light of the event which, as you know, will take place within the next few weeks, have we any intention of opposing the OAU or any plan for provoking hostilities between Angola and other African countries. We wish to be in the concert of African nations. For this reason, we are sending a delegation from MPLA's Political Bureau, which is due to leave for Kampala later today, with the brief of explaining our position to the OAU committee meeting there . . . This time we will not enter once again into the game of manoeuvres which were undertaken during our liberation struggle to bring about a conciliation, in critical times, between the MPLA and the FNLA and, lately, Unita. Therefore, you should not be surprised if the newspapers report the presence of Comrade N'dele, or Comrade Jose Eduardo, in Kampala. They are not going there to take part in the conciliation meeting but, in fact, to explain to the OAU, and especially its chairman General Amin, MPLA's position regarding those two puppet organizations, FNLA and Unita.

With this yet further act in Kampala, we have been able to verify that our enemies, the imperialists, who have tried to divide our movement in the past and who tried to involve us with forces alien to the interests of the people of Angola, still persist and will, no doubt, continue with their activities. We do not think that this OAU initiative is one that is well-intentioned, because it has been preceded by various meetings and rendezvous at which the Angolan question was discussed in our absence. Moreover, as you can see for yourselves, if we were expected right from the outset to take part in this international meeting, it is strange that we should not have been invited to it until last night—that is on the eve of the conference, and this by telephone. Without ever being contacted since the start of the preparations for the meeting, this shows that there exists an intention to present us with a fait accompli, which we surely cannot accept.

[Source= Radio Luanda, 1 October 1975]

Declaration of the Political Bureau of the Central Committee of Unita

Nova Lisboa, 15 October 1975

Where is the legality in the Civil War in Angola?

(1) The civil war which rages today in Angola is an anti-patriotic anti-democratic struggle which Unita has done everything to avoid. It has tried by all means possible to bring the three liberation movements to find a political compromise.

(2) Since 1961, the year when the armed liberation struggle began, the two then existing liberation movements, FNLA and MPLA, began to compete with one another politically and militarily in seeking leadership of Angolan nationalism instead of uniting their efforts for the joint purpose of the country's independence.

(3) The present civil war is only the tragic and unfortunate result of internal quarrels which have followed the long path of the national war of liberation.

(4) Unita does not believe in division and in fratricidal struggles and it made its first appeal for unity in 1966 at its constituent congress on 13 March in Muangai, which is today a historic village for our movement. Our appeal yielded no result because we were considered too small and too weak militarily.

(5) Immediately after the coup d'etat of 25 April 1974, which brought to power in Portugal the regime which began the decolonization of Africa, Unita considered that a valid discussion with the Portuguese Government was impossible without a minimum degree of unity between the three liberation movements.

In spite of the insults, lies and insinuations of which our movement has been the subject on the part of our brothers, we courageously undertook, in a spirit of selflessness and forgetting the past, journeys which took us to Kinshasa where we were to conclude a reconciliation agreement with the FNLA on 16 November 1974 thanks to the patriotic spirit of brother President of the FNLA, Roberto Holden.

We let them know that this act would not be complete if our brothers in the MPLA were not parties to it and that we would be prepared to go to Dar es Salaam for that purpose.

(6) After numerous journeys to Dar es Salaam and Lusaka, we finally succeeded in signing a reconciliation agreement with the MPLA at Luso in Angola on 20 December 1974. After this was done we put forward the idea of a conference of the three liberation movements before starting any talks of any sort with Portugal.

(7) In this way the efforts of Unita resulted in the conference at Mombasa in Kenya on 3 January 1975. We had agreed to set aside our ideological and political differences, but also succeeded in reconciling the FNLA and MPLA and putting in hand a programme of negotiations with Portugal.

(8) Thanks to the Mombasa conference, we succeeded in signing with Portugal on the 15 January 1975, at Alvor, the historic documents which recognizes the right of our people to independence and sets up a coalition government of the three liberation movements which would approve the most democratic formula for holding general

elections before independence and fix the date for independence as 11 November 1975. These victories have been possible thanks to the unity of the three liberation movements.

(9) In March 1975, the first military conflicts arose between the MPLA and FNLA. Unita was concerned to find another compromise for a reconciliation between the three liberation movements. Its efforts resulted in the conference at Nakuru (Kenya) on 10 June 1975. It was called the 'last-chance conference'. We should however pay our respects to the doyen of the struggle in Africa, President Mzee Jomo Kenyatta for acting as a mediator between the three liberation movements.

How is it then that, three weeks after the agreements reached in Nakuru, civil war began in Angola? How did Unita, believing in peace and unity, become involved in the war? What are the prospects for settling this conflict before 11 November, 1975?

The Political Brureau of Unita considered it opportune to prepare this document so as to state its position before the Angolans, before Africa and before the world. The entry of Unita into the war is entirely the fault of the MPLA which has systematically violated all the agreements which have been made, and has attacked the forces of Unita in a cowardly way.

Our troops have been massacred without possibility of defence at: Pica-Pau on 4 June 1975, Gabela 10 June 1975, Lobito 25 June 1975, Cassamba 30 June 1975, Henrique de Carvalho 15 July 1975, Kalabo 22 July 1975, Lukusse 30 July 1975. The aircraft which should have carried brother Savimbi, the President of the movement, was attacked on 5 August 1975 at Silva Porto by the MPLA. As a result of all these acts Unita understood that MPLA had declared war on it. It was necessary to defend itself and to defend the legality of the agreements of Kinshasa, Luso, Mombasa, Alvor and Nakuru.

The responsibility of Portugal, which did not honour its commitments to the three liberation movements, is pregnant with consequences. We are waging war against our will and we are ready to cease fighting immediately in order to begin talking. We have no preliminary conditions for the return of peace to our country and to reconciliation between brothers. Let others answer our appeal and tomorrow there will be no war in Angola.

Our immediate objects are as follows:

(1) To stop the fighting in Angola immediately.

(2) To hold a conference of the three liberation movements with Portugal, neighbouring countries of Angola and observers from UN and OAU so as to find a satisfactory solution to the conflict. Angola must not divide Africa.

(3) To find a provisional solution for 11 November 1975 around a minimum programme for a government of national unity, and to include in this government political and religious leaders of the country who are outside the three liberation movements.

(4) To organize free general elections within eight months after ceasing of military hostilities.

(5) To work for the Unity of the country and its territorial integrity.

(6) To work for national reconciliation of all Angolan brothers.

(7) To work for national reconstruction on a socialist and democratic basis.

(8) To call on international organizations to start the country's economy functioning again.

(9) To compel Portugal to honour its commitments to the three liberation movements, to all Angolans, to Africa and the world as the sole security for its rehabilitation in the concert of nations.

Worse things will happen to our country and SA if:

(a) The MPLA were encouraged in its attempt to make an unilateral declaration of independence. If this happened the other two movements (FNLA and Unita) would have no alternative to declaring that they are the government in turn. Thus, Angola would find itself with two Governments on the eve of its independence and this would necessarily mean the division of the country with unfavourable repercussions at OAU and at world level.

(b) A unilateral declaration of independence by the MPLA would mean that the civil war in Angola becomes established with its procession of misdeeds. The MPLA would never be capable of controlling the immense area of the country and would never succeed in ending the civil war which it has lightly declared.

Every war in Angola is and will always be a war of the countryside where the towns would fall one after the other suffocated by the country people.

(c) The continued war in Angola would not favour the MPLA but it would favour the enemies of national liberation in Africa and the enemies of its unity. Whatever happens to our country on 11 November 1975, Unita will be at its post. On 11 November 1965 a minority of white colonials seized power in Zimbabwe against the will of the black majority. Africa condemned this and it is fighting against it. On 11 November 1975, ten years later, if a handful of men who are thirsty for power should legally seize power in Angola Africa must show this same courage in re-establishing political legality and national reconciliation. At the side of legality is the truth. At the moment they are weak but they will end in triumphing.

OAU Conciliation Commissions Recommendations on Angola Adopted at Kampala on 24 October 1975

Radio Kampala

That an atmosphere of peace and reconciliation be created by the immediate cessation of hostilities in the respective areas under control [of the three liberation movements] on a date to be fixed by the OAU current Chairman, and that the three liberation movements should not advance beyond the position they hold at the time of the proclamation of the ceasefire; that the OAU current Chairman appeals to FNLA, MPLA, and Unita for immediate reconciliation and to immediately conduct consultation among the Heads of State, members of the bureau of the 12th [OAU] summit in Kampala, since the dimensions of the problems of Angola extends beyond the commission's terms of reference; that a government of national union be immediately formed by the three liberation movements for the purpose of leading Angola into independence; that an appeal be made to Portugal to transfer the instrument of independence to the three movements jointly in the event that understanding is not realized before 11 November 1975; that the OAU earnestly appeals to all States, including its members, to immediately cease any interference in the internal affairs of Angola and supplying arms to the parties concerned; in this regard, the three liberation movements must strive to achieve their unity, as this would help to ward off all foreign, African and other interference in the internal affairs of Angola; the condemnation by OAU of the resort to the employment of mercenaries in the supply of arms which are the basic elements for interference in the internal affairs of Angola, which also constitutes factors in the invasion of parts of the Angolan territory by SA, and Rhodesia; the condemnation of SA by the OAU for its aggression against Angola and the invasion of Angola by forces of any other countries whatsoever; That an appeal be made to Portugal by the OAU to withdraw its armed forces from Angola before 11 November 1975; that the three liberation movements should agree among themselves on the holding of elections within twelve months from 11 November 1975; that the OAU takes all necessary measures to prevent any attempt at the internationalization of the Angolan problems, and to extend thanks to all African countries that have contributed their assistance to the liberation movements during the years of struggle for national liberation against Portuguese colonialism.

That the OAU stresses to the liberation movements that if Africa has responsibilities to Angola, the liberation movements, too, have to assume their responsibilities to Africa and that they should consequently review their positions to the OAU.

That no member-State should recognize any liberation movements in the event of the latter declaring unilateral independence . . .

Lourenco Marques Declaration on Angola

Lourenco Marques Radio, 10 November 1975

A one-day meeting of CONCP, Conference of Nationalist Organizations of Portuguese Colonies, convened by the MPLA, PAIGC, MLSTP and Frelimo, ended yesterday [9 November] in Lourenco Marques. The meeting was attended by Samora Moises Machel, Chairman of Frelimo and President of the People's Republic of Mozambique; Agostinho Neto, Chairman of the MPLA; Jose Araujo, member of the Central Committee and the Political Bureau of the PAIGC; and Leonel D'Alva, Minister of Economic Co-ordination of the Government of the Democratic Republic of Sao Tome and Principe, deputizing for President Manuel Costa Pinto. The following is the text of the final declaration of the CONCP meeting:

Representatives of member organizations of CONCP—namely, of the African Party for the Independence of Guinea and Cape Verde, the [Popular] Movement for the Liberation of Angola and the Front for the Liberation of Mozambique—met in Lourenco Marques, capital of Mozambique, on 9 November 1975, at the invitation of Comrade Samora Moises Machel, Chairman of the CONCP. The meeting was convened with the object of studying the grave problem resulting from the imperialist aggression against the Angolan people and their legitimate representative, the MPLA, and to decide on the line of common action, to be taken in solidarity within the framework of the CONCP. Following a detailed report of the Angolan situation by the Chairman of the MPLA, Comrade Agostinho Neto, and speeches by heads of delegations, it was unanimously decided:

(1) That the Republic of Guinea-Bissau, the Republic of Cape Verde, the Democratic Republic of Sao Tome and Principe and the People's Republic of Mozambique, States led by the member-parties of the CONCP, will, on it being so proclaimed by the MPLA, recognize the independent and sovereign State of Angola, in its territorial entirety, and the Government formed by the MPLA.

(2) Vigorously to condemn the imperialist aggression unleashed against the Angolan forces by the lackeys of imperialism, namely SA. This aggression is aimed at putting at stake the total and complete independence of Angola won through 14 years of struggle and sacrifice of the Angolan people, led by the MPLA. It is also aimed at blocking the process of the development of the national liberation struggle in Africa and at destroying the secure rearguard of this combat, represented by African progressive States. It is, therefore, aggression against Africa as a whole.

(3) To denounce the attempt at the recolonization of Angola, carried out by the Portuguese reactionary forces, represented by the so called Portuguese Liberation Army. In this context, to denounce also the use by the puppet organizations, composed of Angolan traitors on the payroll of imperialism, and of Portuguese and other mercenary forces.

(4) To condemn the conduct of the Portuguese Government in Angola's decolonization process, which created the conditions paving the way for the occupation of parts of the territory by foreign forces, thereby constituting complicity in the aggression against the Angolan people.

(5) To reaffirm the solidarity and total support for the party and the struggle of the Angolan people, led by the MPLA, a solidarity founded on the identity of ideas and political objectives, forged between the PAIGC, MLSTP, MPLA and Frelimo, in the long process of the common struggle against colonialism and imperialism.

(6) To call on all peace and freedom-loving nations and all democratic forces of the world to recognize the sovereign State of Angola, its Government and its vanguard, MPLA and to support, with all means, the Angolan people's struggle for the defence of their independence and territorial integrity and their right to progress and peace.

Note. Lourenco Marques (10 November 1975), noting that Aristides Pereira, Secretary-General of the PAIGC and President of Cape Verde, had arrived in

Lourenco Marques on 9 November, said he was too late 'for technical reasons' to attend the CONCP meeting.

Holden Roberto's Proclamation of Independence

AZAP, Kinshasa, 11 November 1975

Mr Holden Roberto proclaimed the independence of the People's Democratic Republic of Angola at midnight, 11 November, in the 15th March Square of Ambriz.

President Holden Roberto, who traced the history of his country's liberation struggle during the past 14 years, called on his compatriots to be vigilant in order to curb the 'appetite of Soviet social-imperialism'. 'The enemies of our people, the latter being docile instruments in the service of ideologies and causes which are foreign to our nature, have imposed fratricidal struggle and criminal and needless sacrifices upon the Angolan people with their Machiavellian slogan of "Luta continua!" and have made Angola into a flaming powder factory,' the FNLA President said.

Concerning the friendly countries which should have been present at the proclamation of independence, the FNLA leader declared that 'all these friends—Zaire, the PRC, Tunisia, the Central African Republic, Nigeria, Ivory Coast, Senegal, Cameroon, Liberia, Uganda, Kenya, Togo, Ghana, Lesotho and other African and Asian States—all these truly friendly countries which know that we are neither acrobats nor Utopians but simply proud nationalists who are attached to the realities of our country—these brothers and friends should know that we are convinced that we can always count on the warmth of their affection'. The FNLA President then said that imperialist interests in Angola are not respectable. 'By this we want to say that we will no longer tolerate our country continuing to be a game reserve, a private estate, a reservoir of raw materials.

'When we say "Freedom and Land", we are thinking of that freedom which would be incomplete without the just distribution of land to those who are living on it,' said Mr Holden Roberto, who added that the FNLA would not practice injustice towards anyone. It should be understood by one and all that it was not only the rich who had the right to eat to their fill, while giving a hypocritical pat on the back of the poor and saying 'We are brothers'.

'True brotherhood is that of heart and sharing. We will therefore proceed to a just and equitable division of the wealth, and only those who have not understood and do not want to understand will feel wronged.' The FNLA President then declared: 'We want to build a new Angola with the assistance of all those who live in it because they love it, without regard to the colour of their skin.' President Holden admitted that Angola was divided at the moment of its accession to independence. 'This is so because, we, the FNLA, can never agree to our country emerging from socio-economic exploitation to come directly under ideological exploitation. That is alienation of the Angolan man's most precious possession—his personality.'

The FNLA President launched an appeal to all Angolan cadres now outside the national territory to return to the country without delay to put their experience at the service of the nation and its people. He said his action programme included a plan for rapid social development of the country by creating new jobs under State protection. In order to abolish the privileged relations of certain existing groups, the FNLA planned social justice and an equitable distribution of the national revenue.

Dr Agostinho Neto's Independence Day Speech

Radio Clube Portugues (Lisbon), 10 November 1975

In the name of the Angolan people, the Central Committee of the Popular Movement for the Liberation of Angola, MPLA, solemnly proclaims the independence of

DOCUMENTS

Angola before Africa and the world. The Angolan people and the Central Committee of the MPLA will now observe one minute of silence and hereby declare that the heroes who fell for the independence of the motherland will live for ever.

Meeting the people's most profound aspirations, the MPLA declares our country constituted into the People's Republic of Angola (*Republica Popular de Angola*). During the period between the signing of the Alvor [Algarve] agreement and the present proclamation, the MPLA alone did not breach the agreements signed. As far as the internal lackeys of imperialism are concerned, we have long since ceased to recognize them as liberation movements. As far as Portugal is concerned, its constant disregard of the Alvor agreements is manifest, among other ways, by the fact that it has systematically remained silent over the invasion of our country by regular armies and mercenary forces. This invasion, already known and reported throughout the world, has not even merited a comment from the Portuguese authorities, who indeed exercised sovereignty only in the areas liberated by the MPLA. Moreover, our movement is facing on the ground a sort of fascist international brigade attacking the Angolan people. Portuguese reactionary forces are included in this alliance and are taking part in the invasion of the south of the country. Yet the Porutgese Government not only has not attacked them but has indeed tacitly encouraged them by its silence and passivity. Despite the fact that the puppet organizations under orders from the invading army have long since been denounced by the Angolan people and by all the world progressive forces, the Portuguese Government insisted on regarding them as liberation movements and attempted to push the MPLA into solutions which would be tantamount to an act of high treason against the Angolan people.

Once more we wish to put on record that our struggle was never, and never will be, against the Portuguese people. On the contrary, from today we shall be in a position to cement fraternal relations between two peoples who share historical and linguistic links, as well as the same goal: freedom . . . Our struggle is not over. Our goal is to achieve our country's complete independence and build a just society and a new man. The fight we are still waging against the lackeys of imperialism, who shall go unnamed in order not to sully this unique moment in our history, is aimed at expelling the foreign invaders, those people who want to establish neo-colonialism in our country. The complete liberation of our country and all our people from foreign oppression is thus the new State's fundamental concern.

Carrying into effect the aspirations of the broad popular masses, the People's Republic of Angola will, under the guidance of the MPLA, gradually advance towards a people's democracy State, with the alliance between workers and peasants as its nucleus . . . The organs of State of the People's Republic of Angola will be under the supreme guidance of the MPLA, and the primacy of the Movement's structures over those of the State will be ensured . . .

With the proclamation of the People's Republic of Angola, the Popular Armed Forces for the Liberation of Angola, FAPLA, are institutionalized as the national army. The FAPLA, the people's armed hand, under the MPLA's firm leadership, are a people's army whose goal is to serve the interests of the most exploited sections of our people. Steeled in the hard struggle of national liberation against Portuguese colonialism, and armed with the revolutionary theory, they remain a fundamental instrument of the anti-imperiaist struggle. As the liberating force of the People's Republic of Angola, the FAPLA will have the task of defending the country's territorial integrity, and, as a people's army, will participate in the great tasks of national reconstruction . . .

On putting an end to colonialism and determinedly barring the way to neo-colonialism, the MPLA declares on this solemn occasion its firm resolve radically to change the present economic infrastructures, and defines from this moment that the goal of economic reconstruction is the satisfaction of the people's needs . . . The People's Republic of Angola will launch increasingly into the industrialization of our own raw materials and even into heavy industry enterprises. However, bearing in mind that most Angolans live off the land, the MPLA has decided to regard agriculture as the basis, and industry as the determining factor, of our progress.

As for private enterprises, even foreign-owned ones, provided that they are useful to the national economy and the interests of the people, they will, on the latter's behalf, be protected and encouraged as laid down in our Movement's broader programme. In its economic relations the People's Republic of Angola will be open to the entire world . . . The MPLA . . . will never betray the sacred principle of national independence. Our international relations will always be in line with the principle of mutual advantage. The People's Republic of Angola will devote particular attention to its relations with Portugal, and, because it wishes them to be lasting ones, it will build them on a new basis, free from any traces of colonialism. The present dispute with Portugal will be approached calmly in order not to poison our future relations. It is evident that, initially, our economy will suffer from a lack of cadres. In order to meet this shortcoming a plan for the rapid training of national cadres will be drawn up, and, at the same time, we shall make an appeal for international co-operation in this sphere . . .

The forces of imperialism do not lay down their arms. Now that we have defeated colonialism, they are intent on imposing on us a new regime of oppression and exploitation through their internal lackeys . . . Our people's revolutionary determination to fight man's exploitation by man, and the differences which separate us from the enemy, demand of us a new war of liberation which will take the form of widespread popular resistance and will have to continue until the final victory. In this context, the productive sector becomes predominant as a battlefront and a basic and vital factor in the advancement of our resistance . . . In order effectively to ensure the support of the glorious FAPLA, the People's Republic of Angola will adopt the measures required to deal with the situation resulting from the invasion of our country. The People's Republic of Angola solemnly reiterates its determination to fight for Angola's territorial integrity, opposing any attempts at dismembering the country.

The People's Republic of Angola sees as a priority and a vital and inalienable task the expulsion from our country of the army made up of SA and Zairean troops, Portuguese fascists, Angolan puppets and mercenaries who represent the combined forces of imperialist aggression against our country . . . The People's Republic of Angola proposes to activate and support the establishment of people's power on a national scale. The working masses will thus exercise power on all levels . . . Another over-riding concern of our State will be the abolition of all forms of discrimination based on sex, age, ethnic or racial origin, or religion, and the strict observance of the just principle of equal pay for equal work . . .

The People's Republic of Angola declares itself a lay State, with complete separation between the Church and the State, respecting all religions and protecting all the churches, places and objects of worship and legally recognized institutions: The People's Republic of Angola, aware of its importance and responsibilities in the southern African and world contexts, reiterates its solidarity with all the world's oppressed peoples, especially the peoples of Zimbabwe and Namibia struggling against racist domination . . .

Having achieved national independence, the MPLA and the Angolan people wish to express their heartfelt gratitude for the help rendered by all the friendly peoples and countries to our heroic national liberation struggle. Our gratitude goes to all the African peoples and countries who remained on our side, to the socialist countries, to the Portuguese revolutionary forces, and to the progressive organizations and governments of Western countries who understood and supported the Angolan people's struggle.

The sovereign People's Republic of Angola will maintain diplomatic relations with all the world countries based on the principles of mutual respect, national sovereignty, non-interference, respect for territorial integrity, non-aggression, equality, reciprocity of benefits and peaceful co-existence.

The People's Republic of Angola, a free and independent African State, voices its adherence to the principles of the OAU Charter and the UN Charter. The foreign policy of the People's Republic of Angola, based on the principle of total independence observed by the MPLA from the outset, will be one of non-alignment.

The People's Republic of Angola will respect its international undertakings, and, equally, the international routes using its territory. The People's Republic of Angola, a country committed to the anti-imperialist struggle, will have as natural allies the African countries, the socialist countries and all the world progressive forces.

Comrades, on this moment when the Angolan people are covered in glory thanks to the victories and sacrifices of their best sons, we greet in the People's Republic of Angola, our first State, the liberation of our beloved motherland. From Cabinda to the Cunene, united in the common motherland, in the blood shed in the cause of freedom, we pay tribute to the heroes who fell in five long centuries of resistance, and shall be worthy of their example. We respect the characteristics of each region, of each populational nucleus of our country, for all of us equally offer the motherland the sacrifices its survival demands . . . United from Cabinda to the Cunene, we shall vigorously carry on the widespread popular resistance, and shall build our democratic and popular State. Honour to the new Angolan man; eternal glory to our heroes; the struggle continues; victory is certain; victory is certain.

Kinshasa Agreement between FNLA and Unita

Excerpts from Lisbon Radio, 11 November 1975

Protocol of agreement between the liberation movements FNLA, the National Front for the Liberation of Angola, and Unita, the National Union for the Total Independence of Angola:

On 10 November the FNLA and Unita signed the present agreement defining the provisional framework of power in Angola which the legitimate representatives of the Angolan people deem their bounden duty to lay down on the occasion of their solemn accession to independence.

Considering that the Popular Movement for the Liberation of Angola, MPLA, has refused every opportunity to achieve a platform of understanding and deliberately chose to try to take power by force, the two movements FNLA and Unita, aware that they represent the majority of the people of almost all of Angola, have decided in view of the present circumstances to publish a constitutional act to introduce the necessary changes to the basic laws of the country to define the organs of political power which will exercise political power in the Republic of Angola.

It is further agreed that the FNLA will appoint the President of the Council of the Revolution, and Unita will appoint the Prime Minister of the Government of Angola. The FNLA will further appoint the Commander under whom the National Defence Command will operate. It is further agreed that the appointment of the provincial governors will be made by means of consultations between the two liberation movements in keeping with the equal footing laid down in the constitutional act. The two movements undertake to devote all their efforts to strengthening the ties established on a common politico-military front which will lead to more efficient government of the country.

Signed in Kinshasa, on 10 November 1975, on behalf of the President of the FNLA, by Johnny Pinnock Eduardo, member of the Political Bureau, and, on behalf of the President of Unita, by Jose N'dele, member of the Political Bureau.

AFRICA
CONTEMPORARY RECORD

Annual Survey and Documents

VOL 9 1976/77

Edited by COLIN LEGUM

"Of all the many works of reference devoted to Africa, this is the only one worth buying in its latest edition year after year." *The Economist*

Combining scholarly accuracy with journalistic timeliness, Volume 9 includes essays on the following:

- Dr. Kissinger's diplomacy and the turbulent political developments in Southern Africa.
- The recent policies and underlying concerns of the Soviet Union and China in Africa.
- The East African community in crisis and the threat of dissolution.
- The Organization of African Unity in a year of intense conflict and change.
- The Cuban presence in strife-torn Angola.
- Afro-Arab relations and the summit meeting of 1977.

as well as:

- 54 country-by-country surveys of the year's events in each of Africa's nations and territories.
- More than 80 documents relating to the politcal, economic and social developments in Africa.

ca. 1200 pp. / ISBN 0-8419-0158-9 / 1977

Vols. 1-8, covering the years 1968-1976, are available.
Standing orders are invited.

AFRICANA PUBLISHING COMPANY
A division of Holmes & Meier Publishers, Inc.
30 Irving Place, New York, N.Y. 10003